I0885789

Between Myths and Margins

Sociology of Race and Ethnicity

Between Myths and Margins

Gendered Racist Microaggressions as Everyday Racism

Dresden N. Lackey

The University of Georgia Press
ATHENS

Sociology of Race and Ethnicity web page

Published by the University of Georgia Press
Athens, Georgia 30602
www.ugapress.org

Set in 10.5/13.5 Garamond Premier Pro Regular
by Westchester Publishing Services

Printed digitally

EU Authorized Representative
Easy Access System Europe—Mustamäe tee 50, 10621
Tallinn, Estonia, gpsr.requests@easproject.com

Library of Congress Control Number: 2026006393
ISBN: 9780820375755 (paperback)
ISBN: 9780820375748 (hardback)
ISBN: 9780820375762 (ebook)
ISBN: 9780820375779 (PDF)

CONTENTS

CHAPTER 1. "You're One of *Those*": Microaggressions and Macroimplications 1

CHAPTER 2. Theoretical Perspectives on Microaggressions and Everyday Racism 15

CHAPTER 3. Moving Toward Whiteness 25

CHAPTER 4. The Right and Wrong Kind 45

CHAPTER 5. Body Talk 59

CHAPTER 6. The Role of Internalized Racism in Interracial Microaggressions 71

CHAPTER 7. Compliments of the (White) House 77

CHAPTER 8. White Women: Oppression Olympics, White Saviors, and Controlling Images 93

CHAPTER 9. White Sexual Imperialism and White Men 111

CHAPTER 10. "It's Ontological": Moving Forward in Understanding Microaggressions 125

ACKNOWLEDGMENTS 131

NOTES 133

INDEX 149

Between Myths and Margins

CHAPTER 1

"You're One of *Those*"

Microaggressions and Macroimplications

At the end of the first year of my PhD program, I attended a party to celebrate the granting of tenure to two women of color faculty mentors. As I was relatively new to the department, there were many students from prior cohorts in attendance that I had not met. One student, a white woman, introduced herself to me and asked a question I have been asked (and I will bet every other Asian American living in the United States has been asked) perhaps more times than any other question in my life: "Where are you from?"

I have always answered this question the same way, though the reasons why I choose this response have certainly changed. I grew up in Asheville, North Carolina: a predominantly white, ostensibly progressive small city nestled in the Appalachian Mountains. As a child, "Asheville" was my answer to this question simply because it was true; my family moved to Asheville when I was a toddler, and I grew up in the same house until I left for college. By my early twenties, I had been asked this question—and undergone the same follow-up questions to my unchanging response—enough times to know what the inquirer truly meant by those four seemingly innocuous words. As an adult, "Asheville" was my answer to give the stranger a chance to reconsider their assumption, to accept my answer as fact, and move on. They rarely did.

"No, where are you *really* from? You look some kind of Asian!" this student asked with wide eyes. When I explained that my mom is Korean but that I grew up in Asheville, the student asked if my father had been in the military, stationed in South Korea, when my parents met. This was true.

"So you're one of *those*," she said, nodding with satisfaction that her assumption was correct. "There are a lot of you."

Research Questions

I initially designed this project to examine the ways in which regional boundaries impact the microaggressions that Black and Asian women receive. I have lived in four different southeastern states, and I am often asked what it's like to navigate the South as a nonwhite woman. This question always gives me pause, as I recount the experiences of microaggressive racism I have witnessed in all regions I have visited in the United States and outside of it, hardly exclusive to the American South. This project began as a quest to address that assumption: Is the Southeast really *that* much more racist than the Northeast? Or does racism just look different depending on the region? But ultimately, my question became, who cares? Is one necessarily kinder than the other? More digestible? Less harmful? Who cares if racism is overt or covert and where, if they are merely two sides of the same coin?

While conducting interviews during the onset of COVID-19, it was necessary to modify my methodology from in-person interviews to online, which allowed me to expand my respondent pool. As I began to understand further the ways in which white supremacy does not care which states were technically below the Mason-Dixon Line, I modified the goals of this project to better understand not just how microaggressions operate on the micro level for Black and Asian American women in the United States, but also how they reaffirm white supremacist patriarchy across borders, across time zones, and across community settings.

The research questions that guided my project are as follows:

- Who are the perpetrators of microaggressions against Asian American and Black women?
- Do Black and Asian women experience distinct microaggressions depending on the race and gender of the perpetrator?
- How can microaggressions against women of color inform us about the ways in which white supremacist patriarchy operates?
- How can we understand microaggressions within the larger context of structural racism?

To address these questions, I revisit my background in psychology to examine the current discourse around microaggressions and how that discourse can be in conversation with my current home discipline of sociology. By utilizing perspectives in both fields, we can better understand gendered racist microaggressions as products of a broader white supremacy rather than as single incidents of racism enacted by individual actors.

Understanding Microaggressions

Critical race theorist Derrick Bell describes the concept of *racial realism*: Racism is permanent and does not improve nor dissipate; rather, it changes form to adapt to modern times.[1] White supremacy today is less often the white hoods and lynchings it once was; nor is it segregated water fountains or federal internment camps. However, the lack of formal segregation, blatant name-calling, and exclusionary laws do not reflect racism's end; both in past and present, a long-standing white supremacist ideology creates and maintains the power and resources that support racial prejudice institutionally and interpersonally.[2]

Although racism today is perhaps often less overt than blatant enslavement or legal segregation, whites and people of color alike have adapted a neoliberal ideology that criticizes and discredits the significance of race, hiding behind a "color-blind" meritocracy platform alleging that all people have equal opportunity to succeed in the American Dream, regardless of how they are racialized.[3] Thus, considering Bell's notion of racial realism, it is imperative to understand and expose the hidden, strategic nature of how oppressions manifest in modern times and how individual actions reinstate the perpetual social force of white supremacy.

One of those modern manifestations is the microaggression. Microaggressions describe subtle remarks and actions directed at marginalized groups that reinforce their oppression but do not seem inherently prejudiced on the surface.[4] The perpetrator of a microaggression may base these comments or actions on another's race, sexuality, ability, gender, class, or other marginalized identity, often operating at multiple sites. Microaggressions are subtle enough to leave the receiver wondering, "Did I take that comment the wrong way?" or "Was the slight all in my head?"

Even years after the exchange with my fellow graduate student and years of formally studying microaggressions since, I still wonder what she meant by that comment as it rings through my ears verbatim: "You're one of *those*. There are a lot of you." A lot of children of ex-military fathers? A lot of mixed-race children? Did she specifically mean children with a Korean mother and white father? Or more broadly, an Asian mother and white father? How is "a lot" measured? A lot compared to whom? Unlike overt racist comments and behaviors, microaggressions leave room for interpretation, frequently agonizing the receiver for days, months, or years after the exchange. Whereas hate crimes or demeaning slurs are socially chastised, the subtlety of microaggressions allow them to remain protected under the innocuousness of color blindness.

Sociologists and race scholars have studied countless nooks and crannies of racism: color-blind racism, systemic racism, coloniality and imperialism, internalized racism, legal racism—the list goes on. Central to each of these iterations of oppression is the understanding that in the United States, racism is white domination and white supremacy. Research on racist microaggressions are no different; from the inception of the microaggression concept by Chester Pierce in the 1970s to the resurgence of attention microaggressions received after psychologist Derald Wing Sue's creation of microaggression taxonomy in the early 2000s, microaggression research has grown across disciplines, settings, and identity categories. What is missing, however, is the connection between microaggressions and white supremacy as a structure: the situating of the micro to macro.[5]

Microaggressions as Everyday Racism

Fundamental to microaggression discourse are the contributions of psychiatrist Chester Pierce. Considered the father of microaggression research, Pierce coined the term in 1970 in his landmark chapter, "Offensive Mechanisms." In contrast to the widely studied psychiatric phenomenon of *defense* mechanisms that are primarily engaged by those aiming to reduce shame and guilt, Pierce described *offensive* mechanisms as subtle, incessant blows, ultimately rooted in violence and aggression. Enacted by white perpetrators onto Black recipients, Pierce conceptualized offensive mechanisms such as microaggressions as automatic, conscious, unconscious, or preconscious, and serve "as a vehicle for the micro-aggressive episodes that come to total up racism."[6]

Pierce thus acknowledges that racist experiences exist along a spectrum from overt to covert, obvious to subtle, indisputable to deniable. As racial realism demonstrates, there is not one singular definition or checklist for what makes an act racist per se. Crucial to comprehending racism as a structure is unpacking the ways in which micro and macro interact; though an individual act may or may not be clearly labeled as racist, the culmination of everyday interactions ultimately acquiesce to larger social forces that both maintain and incentivize white supremacy over time.

Although the United States is no stranger to frequent civilian hate crimes, racially motivated mass shootings, and police violence disproportionately targeting Black and brown people, arguably all people of color experience racism daily through more subtle means. The nature of racial realism is that in any given time, racism takes a variety of forms, ranging in magnitude from covert to overt. Like Pierce, critical social theorist Philomena Essed recognized the underlying racist significance in subtle, seemingly unracialized comments and behaviors enacted onto people of color. She referred to the cumulation of these slights as *everyday racism*: incidents of injustice that recur so frequently that they become an expected certainty of one's everyday life.[7]

Three strands of everyday racism create mutually dependent processes that demonstrate how micro and macro are both at play: the *marginalization* of people of color, the *problematization* of nonwhite cultures and identities, and the *repression* of their resistance to white supremacy.[8] Marginalizing people of color ensures they are viewed as problems to and of society, and any potential resistance is thwarted to ensure they remain subordinated under the domination of whiteness. In defining her theory, Essed distinguishes that "everyday racism is racism, but not all racism is everyday racism."[9] She critiques the belief that racism is strictly structural, or that it is strictly interpersonal, and instead argues that the structural ideology of racism is reinforced through the everyday mundane practice of individuals. Racism, then, may generally refer to a broad ideology that upholds white domination over people of color, but it is the ease with which that ideology seeps into routine everyday situations, interactions, and behaviors that maintains the structural force of white supremacy.

Essed's work is crucial in recognizing the cyclicality of micro and macro social facts, noting that "each instantiation of everyday racism has meaning only in relation to the whole complex of relations and practices."[10] Although my encounter with the graduate student at the party was a single exchange between the two of us, it was a brick in the larger wall of everyday racist microaggressions I had experienced up until that point, and on that brick are layers more that I have experienced in the years since, held together with the mortar of racialized othering as a tool of white domination. This exchange was much more than the four words she spoke without hesitation, the follow-up questions that felt like an interrogation, or the othering she enacted with an assumptive nod and smile. To her, the question was one that anyone may ask a stranger at a party. But the relationship this micro-interaction, and so many others, has to the macro social force of white supremacy is the crux of what must be examined.

Although Essed does not use the same nomenclature that Pierce does when describing commonplace racist behaviors and comments between whites and people of color, there are obvious similarities between their scholarship.[11] Both microaggressions and everyday racism are concepts that refer to common, ordinary behaviors that are routine and unremarkable on the surface but ultimately maintain structural racism. Pierce and Essed both emphasize the cumulative effect of such routine interactions between individuals, and both utilize the experiences of Black people (Pierce's patients, Essed's respondents) to strengthen their theories.[12] And perhaps most important, fundamental to both scholars' theories is the acknowledgment of and emphasis placed on the mutual interdependence of racism's micro and macro components.

Thus, throughout *Between Myths and Margins*, I refer to microaggressions as a type of everyday racism. My respondents discuss experiences that are both specific and broad. They frequently shared stories of particular microaggressions they witnessed, stories like my own at the party, stories where microaggressions cut so deeply that they can still hear the exact inflection of the comment despite the time that has passed. But along with these distinct memories, respondents also shared general covert messages that they witnessed over time: not necessarily distinct events but rather messages that, like microaggressions, are not ostensibly discriminatory yet have veiled inferences rooted in perpetuating gendered racism.

Such incidents of mundane everyday racism meet the criteria of microaggressions as well. In *Offensive Mechanisms*, Pierce provides examples of microaggressive occurrences that are not only individual incidents but also the accumulation of several incidents that send a consistent message. Such is the nature of something routine; like putting gas in your car or buying bread at the store, the experience is so commonplace that despite knowing it occurred, every unique event becomes quite unremarkable. Even so, the cumulation of such occurrences sends an imposing message about white domination and the inferior status of Black and Asian women. Those accounts are also shared in the coming chapters.

White Supremacy as a Macro Social Force

White supremacy is a macro social force that exalts the colonialist and imperialist agenda of empire on the basis of race. The concept of race, though not a biological or genomic reality, is a social construct born from racism that has very real and tangible consequences. White supremacist ideology legitimizes the power and wealth associated with whiteness through an adoption of systemic racism and a white racial dominant framework. It is important to acknowledge white supremacy not as a collection of individual people's acts but as a dominant social system that shapes the lives of all people living within that system.[13]

As an instrument of white supremacy, anti-Blackness operates not necessarily to elevate whiteness but instead to degrade Blackness. Anti-Blackness ensures that the legacy of enslavement, colonialism, and empire continue to diminish the value of Black lives. Further, anti-Blackness shapes the lives on non-Black people of color as well. Anti-Black ideology allows non-Black groups to subscribe to the justification of white supremacy—they may not reap all of the benefits of whiteness, but at least they are not Black. Political scientist Claire Jean Kim explains, "Whites, then, are lifted up by both white supremacy and anti-Blackness, and Black people are pushed down by both. All other groups, including Asian Americans, are simultaneously *pushed down by white supremacy and lifted up by anti-Blackness*."[14]

White supremacy is thereby not a structure that operates in one singular way on all people of color. Rather, its adaptability is what makes it a tool that can be used against people of color by whites and also against people of color by other people of color who have internalized white supremacist ideologies. We can reason, then, that not only are women of color victimized by white supremacy but can become complicit in it as well. I chose to interview Black and Asian American women for this reason; their racialized histories within the United States are both distinct yet parallel. This research is not meant to be a comparative analysis between Black and Asian women but a study of the multidimensional operatives of white supremacy through everyday racism.

What's So Macro About Microaggressions?

To regard racial microaggressions solely as behaviors or comments between individuals discounts the role of white supremacy as a societal structure that affirms and reaffirms itself through everyday behavior. It is important to credit Pierce with defining the root of microaggressions as, in fact, macro; he approached the interpersonal nature of microaggressions as dependent on feelings of superiority that are ultimately justified and legitimized by white supremacist ideological thinking.[15] Unfortunately, much of Pierce's foundational conceptualization of microaggressions has been largely overlooked in more recent discourse, instead invoking the early 2000s resurgence of racial microaggression scholarship headed by psychologist Derald Wing Sue that centralizes the interpersonal interactions of microaggressions independently. Since the early 2000s, microaggression scholarship has typically acknowledged Pierce as the founder of the term but disregards his additional work on the subject including major components of the concept.[16] His work is often cited but rarely thoroughly engaged with, and consequently, the structural component of microaggressions has been too often abandoned.[17]

To date, most current research on microaggressions is housed in the fields of psychology, counseling, and education and has focused on the interpersonal (micro) nature of microaggressive exchanges.[18] This is not surprising, considering *micro* is, after all, the prefix of the term. Critiques of the terminology "microaggression" suggest that the word minimizes the heavy psychological impact of interpersonal interactions, and microaggression scholarship has often been misconceptualized to support this belief.[19] However, when naming microaggressions in his original conception, Pierce did not minimize the repercussions of everyday racism. Instead, he recognized these behaviors as those that "ignored, tyrannized, terrorized, and minimized" their targets, noting that microaggressions "are only micro in name, since their very number requires a total effort that is incalculable."[20] His use of the prefix *micro-* reflects an acknowledgment of everyday, ordinary racism in contrast to less frequent (and more overt) racist events, in agreement with Essed's conceptualization of everyday racism. Yet, the erasure of Pierce's extensive work in recent microaggression discourse contributes to the lost understanding of this important interdependence.

As demonstrated in the following chapters, gendered racist microaggressions are much more than exchanges between individuals. Racism is not confined to individual exchanges, nor is it confined to institutions. It is not solely about the psychological and emotional impact on a target, nor the intention of the perpetrator. We must question what these interpersonal interactions tell us about our society at large and about the process by which unequal relations of power are maintained. What makes a microaggression more than just a comment or behavior between people? Why, as microaggression discourse becomes more mainstream, do we still feel the sting of microaggressions years after the fact? The social force within which the microaggressions are given power is what allows them to remain relevant; regardless of whether our friends, colleagues, or neighbors learn to watch their microaggressions around people of color, attend diversity workshops, and join anti-racist book clubs, white supremacist patriarchy does not dissipate.

There is a thread that ties all microaggression experiences together. To study microaggressions as solely microlevel episodes is to view a social phenomenon with one eye closed. Microaggressions are merely one shade of brick that contribute to the larger wall of a white supremacist, patriarchal structure. The absence of a structural focus within microaggression discourse is not simply a gap in existing research; this emphasis on micro interactions neglects the influence that macro (structural) forces have on *every* interpersonal interaction. Individual actions and behaviors that reflect racism, as well as sexism, heterosexism, and other prejudices, do not hold oppressive power without the ideological beliefs in white supremacy and heteropatriarchy that serve to justify them.[21] We do not exist in a vacuum; our individual behaviors, beliefs, and preferences are shaped by the society within which we live.

Racists-with-a-Capital-R

Part of what allows microaggressions to be so ordinary that they are easy to disregard is that they distance perpetrators from the label of *racist*, yet still uphold white domination. Ask anyone in the United States what comes to mind when they hear the term "racist" and they will list the obvious: white hoods, derogatory names, hate crimes. They may even name the slightly less overt: police profiling and brutality, immigration or travel bans, and so-called Karens.[22] These are tenets that easily mark a person or policy with the label of what I call *Racist-with-a-capital-R*. Ask the same people if they consider themselves racists: they will tell you, of course not. They are not using derogatory racist language, and they may even vote in favor of open borders, rally against voter suppression, and attend every Black Lives Matter protest in their city. They may have read Ibram X. Kendi's *Stamped from the Beginning* or Robin DiAngelo's *White Fragility*, and they may repost infographics about Juneteenth every year on their social media pages. They cannot be racist because they are not Racist-with-a-capital-R.

It is easy for people to see themselves as accountable, good, and even anti-racist when they are not engaging in behavior that would grant them the label of Racist-with-a-capital-R. But as Shannon Sullivan attests, "white liberals and white supremacists are not as different as white liberals would like to believe and would like others to believe. They grow from the same tree of white domination, . . . and this means that many of the 'anti-racist' habits, practices, and beliefs of the white liberal also are rooted in and help nourish white racism."[23]

In progressive spaces, Racist-with-a-capital-R behavior can be labeled as such and then dismissed as ignorant and hateful rhetoric conducted by ignorant and hateful people. The goal of such behavior is undoubtedly the supremacy of the white race. Yet, microaggressions and other forms of everyday racism utilize a different method to achieve the same end goal, regardless of whether that goal is explicitly stated. That goal is still white domination. Through quotidian backhanded compliments, racialized othering, offhanded slights, and even body language, communicating the superiority of whiteness becomes so routine that it is not even noticed by the perpetrators. As long as their behavior distances themselves from the label of Racist-with-a-capital-R, they do not risk having to be accountable for upholding white domination. The impact of their actions does not matter because the intent was not aligned with Racists-with-a-capital-R. Their actions may have even been unconscious or preconscious.[24] Unless addressed outright, microaggressions thus go disregarded by their perpetrators given that they are not what comes to mind when most people think of racism. This enables perpetrators to continue feeling good about their anti-racist efforts since they are not like Racists-with-a-capital-R and would never behave in ways that would brand them as such. Chester Pierce himself describes this social habit in plain language: "Almost all oppressors are unmindful of the withering effects of cumulative, individual, and collective microaggressions toward victims, even honestly believing that they themselves have inflicted no damage upon socially devalued persons."[25]

Microaggression Research in Sociology

Microaggression research has expanded across fields in recent years, including within the field of sociology. Still, much of microaggression research within sociology focuses on interpersonal interactions rather than meso and macro social forces, echoing the approaches in education, psychology, and psychiatry. In May 2017, *Sociological Inquiry* published a special issue on racial microaggressions that included research on Black, First Nations, and Latinx populations. In the opening article, Embrick, Domínguez, and Karsak outline sociology's contribution to racial microaggression research as essential.[26] They note the lack of attention in psychology research to the structural conditions that allow microaggressions to flourish and how, as sociologists "understand that social inequality and racial inequality are structured, reproduced, and challenged at all levels—micro, meso, and macro," extending microaggression theory to sociological perspectives will offer a more complete, holistic, and structural understanding of microaggressive behaviors, actions, and slights.[27] In a later article, Domínguez and Embrick propose that studying microaggressions through a sociological framework will create a focus on the (macro) root causes of everyday racism "rather than trying to figure out how to bandage the victims of racial violence," and call for an emphasis on Essed's pivotal works on everyday racism.[28] Still, sociological research surrounding microaggressions has primarily relied on Sue's taxonomy, rooted in psychological theory. The analysis presented in this book was largely inspired by calls to eradicate this erasure of Pierce and the lack of attention to structure in sociological understandings of gendered racist microaggressions.

Positionality of the Researcher

In recognition of feminist theory and methodology, it is important to acknowledge my own positionality as a sociologist and researcher. I am a biracial Korean American, straight, cisgender woman who has largely resided in Southeastern cities of the United States. The daughter of a Korean immigrant, I was raised in a predominantly white city and was often the only nonwhite person in my classrooms, places of work, group of friends, and after my parents' divorce, even my family home. My own understanding of gendered racist microaggressions comes from firsthand experience. Although not entirely unexpected, many of the respondents' stories—Black and Asian alike—paralleled my own: feeling consistently, perpetually, incurably like an outsider within, regardless of whether the space was *white* space.

It was important to me to conduct this research with Black and Asian American women, not as a comparative effort but as a collaborative one. My identity as a non-Black woman of color uniquely positions me as both historically marginalized and societally viewed as "the model minority."[29] Although I have experienced anti-Asian racism, I have simultaneously been protected from the anti-Blackness that has plagued the spaces I have visited and lived. Further, anti-Blackness in Asian communities and vice versa is no secret in the history of U.S. race relations; it was necessary for me to communicate with respondents that I would not deny, diminish, or minimize their encounters with such racism and that they could speak freely about such experiences, even in the event that the perpetrators were members of my own co-ethnic group.

In an effort to acknowledge white supremacy as the hand controlling the tensions between Black and Asian communities in the United States, a primary goal for all of my research is to build solidarity among Black and Asian American women. As mine and others' research confirms, microaggressions change depending on the identities of the perpetrator and those of the receiver due to differences in racialized and gendered histories. And still, the underlying cause, the dominating structures from which they are given the power to feel like a thousand cuts, remains consistent regardless of the receiver. To build solidarity among these groups is to both recognize those differences and find commonality and compassion within them. Filipina American sociologist Victoria Reyes describes my own position perfectly:

> Although I am not a Black feminist, cannot produce Black Feminist Thought, and do not experience the world and systems of oppression in the same way as Black women, acceptance of the messiness of life, structural positions as outsiders, deep concern with how these positions and accompanying lived experiences are shaped by broader structures, and calls for solidarity and to act with integrity all speak to me. I find parallels between my life and those writings, conversations, and friendships with Black feminist scholars. In their spaces, I am honored to be a guest. I feel welcomed despite, or maybe because of, my differences.[30]

My status as formally educated, a U.S. citizen, light skinned, able-bodied, and a fluent English speaker afford me privileges over many of my respondents. Yet, being a nonwhite woman and a first-generation college graduate permitted me an insider status with each of my respondents as well. This insider status was sometimes presumed and sometimes slowly earned throughout our time together. My respondents' sincerity, vulnerability, and humor throughout their conversations with me, often a stranger prior to our interviews, shaped my own perception of solidarities among women of color as well.

Although microaggression research has substantially been studied by scholars of psychology, to pay respect to Pierce's original work, we must expand the micro focus if we want to understand *why* microaggressions hurt at an individual level. With graduate degrees in both psychology and sociology, I feel uniquely privileged to study microaggressions with insight in each field. My love for teaching and research was born in psychology departments and I am grateful to my early mentors who guided and encouraged the researcher in me. Coming to sociology fostered the practice of thinking beyond the individual and to examine the influence of power and domination on everyday life. *Between Myths and Margins* would not have been written without the influence and support of my mentors in both disciplines.

Overview

Chapter 2 explores the theoretical foundations within which this research is situated. I first discuss systemic racism theory and the white racial frame as conceptualized by Joe Feagin and tie these to color-blind racism as outlined by Eduardo Bonilla-Silva. I then discuss intersectionality, controlling images, and the matrix of domination as conceptualized by Patricia Hill Collins. Finally, I discuss the importance of everyday racism and critical race feminism.

Chapters 3–6 comprise the unit that examines microaggressions perpetrated by intraracial group members. In chapter 3, I focus on the gendered racist microaggression experiences that reflect a desire for whiteness by co-ethnic communities. The desire to be proximate to whiteness, the pathologizing of nonwhite culture, and attempts to imitate whiteness are all described here. In chapter 4, respondents identify their experiences with defining Blackness and Asianness and how they achieved or failed to be the "right" and "wrong" kind of Black or Asian. In chapter 5, respondents discuss their bodies as extensions of "right" and "wrong" kinds—how their bodies are read, sexualized, and criticized by white standards of beauty. The microaggressions outlined in these chapters were perpetuated by friends, family members, peers, and strangers of the respondent's own ethnicity. I outline the specific themes of microaggressions that Black and Asian American women received in co-ethnic spaces, and in chapter 6, I examine the ways in which internalized racism account for these experiences.

Chapters 7–9 shift to gendered racist microaggressions enacted by white perpetrators onto Black and Asian American women. Chapter 7 shares three case studies of women who were raised in predominantly white households and outline the unique themes of microaggressions perpetrated in these settings. In chapter 8, I highlight the specific gendered racist microaggressions enacted by white women perpetrators, whether coworkers, friends, or strangers. Chapter 9 describes those perpetrated by white men.

In the final chapter, I review the themes of gendered racist microaggressions that my research revealed and discuss the focus on resilience and resistance strategies as coping mechanisms of experiencing everyday racism. I critique the call for victims of gendered racist microaggressions to exercise resilience and coping, which again focuses on microlevel band-aids for macrolevel social problems and negates accountability of perpetrators.

Conclusion

Between Myths and Margins exposes the interdependent relationship between gendered racist microaggressions and macro social forces, drawing from thirty-five in-depth interviews with self-identifying Black and Asian American women. In agreement with feminist theories, this project enters the lived experiences of these historically marginalized groups and recognizes their experiences as truth. Asian American respondents ethnically identified as Korean American, Filipino American, Taiwanese/Japanese, Vietnamese American, Chinese, Indian, Vietnamese/Chinese/Pacific Islander, and Taiwanese/Singaporean. Although some respondents immigrated to the United States as young children, I utilize the broad terminology "Asian American" to distinguish between respondents who were raised in the United States and those who were not and do not identify necessarily as American. Black respondents ethnically identified as ADOS (American descendants of slaves), Guyanese, Guyanese/Trinidadian, Nigerian, Botswanan, and Caribbean.

In situating this work sociologically, I use an intersectional, critical race feminist, and systemic racism framework to explore how Asian American and Black women experience gendered racist microaggressions within and outside of their intraracial communities, highlighting the role that a white racial framework plays in the perpetuation and maintenance of everyday racism. Understanding microaggressions through an intersectional lens contributes to a more complete understanding of the nuance in how everyday racism is executed against women of color.

This research extends the theories outlined by Feagin, Pierce, and Essed by importing the existing work of microaggressions that has largely lived in the field of psychology into a sociological, intersectional, and critical race feminist framework.[31] This research further supports Feagin's argument that racism and the white racial frame are so historically embedded within the United States that they are inescapable even within communities of color.[32] Using a critical race feminist approach, this book reveals how racialized gendered microaggressions are perpetrated against Black and Asian American women—two groups that have quite unique sexualized and gendered type differences in microaggression experiences. As racism and white supremacy continue to adapt through neoliberal and color-blind ideologies, examining its ever-changing nature allows marginalized groups to resist through the legitimizing of their unique lived experiences and the creation of counterframes.

CHAPTER 2

Theoretical Perspectives on Microaggressions and Everyday Racism

Research on the psychological and long-term impacts of microaggressions on people of color and others with marginalized identities elucidates the obvious: that microaggressions, "little murders," or "death by a thousand cuts" are much more than just the incident at hand.[1] But perhaps less obvious is that they are also more than their cumulative effect on individuals or communities. Yes, microaggressions are harmful to individuals, but the individual is not where the harm begins and ends; they are also by-products of a larger phenomenon that has been largely disregarded in microaggression discourse.

Sociologists conceptualize such phenomena through theory. Theory is not always easy to grasp, but it binds microaggression experiences to one another and back to macro social forces. In *Teaching to Transgress: Education as the Practice of Freedom*, bell hooks writes, "I came to theory desperate, wanting to comprehend—to grasp what was happening around and within me. Most importantly, I wanted to make the hurt go away. I saw in theory then a location for healing."[2] In sociology, theory allows us to understand patterns and behaviors of society; it allows us to share language and experiences and to understand cause and effect. But as hooks notes, theory can also be liberatory if we ask it to be. It can be a site of resistance and a site of healing. Theory can be a weapon with which we dismantle oppressive structures. Solving microaggressions is not about calling out perpetrators, intervening at the time of the event, or diversity, equity, and inclusion trainings. Eradicating microaggressions is about dismantling white supremacy.

Systemic Racism, the White Racial Frame, and Color Blindness

In the opening sentence of his monumental text *The Racial Contract*, philosopher Charles W. Mills notes in plain language, "White supremacy is the unnamed political system that has made the modern world what it is today."[3] Within the context of the United States, where the research in this book was situated, racism operates as white supremacy wherein whites maintain racial dominance and power over all people of color. White supremacy, white ideology, and the normalization of white dominance is not incidental; rather, its perpetuation is constructed, intentional, and invested in by whites and nonwhites alike.[4]

One of the greatest myths of white supremacy is that it lives solely within hateful individuals. Kwame Ture and Charles Hamilton argue instead that white supremacy exists, both when a Black Birmingham church is intentionally bombed by hateful individuals but also within the deaths of hundreds to thousands of Black children who do not survive poverty, poor medical treatment, and discrimination in the same town.[5] A single cruel person's actions may not have directly contributed to those thousands of deaths per se, but the culmination of individual support for anti-Black policy and economic power did. Ture and Hamilton describe this as *institutional racism*: structured racial practices that legitimize white political-economic power and affirm ideologies of a racial hierarchy within which whiteness dominates. With rose-colored glasses, we can pretend that if we remove all the white hoods, the bombed churches, and the individual members of terrorist organizations from a society, racism would be solved. This daydream that many believe in allows individuals to absolve themselves from being labeled as Racist-with-a-capital-R. But that is not the society we live in. Instead, everyday people who would never bomb a church or put on the white hood or even use a racist slur behind closed doors, and thus would never see themselves as a racist, still vote for racist policies and subscribe to racist attitudes and ideologies that maintain the racialized status quo of anti-Blackness and white domination in society. This is how institutional racism perseveres.

Inspired by the works of Frederick Douglass, Ida B. Wells-Barnett, W. E. B. Du Bois, and other activist-scholars, sociologist Joe Feagin outlines the theory of systemic racism, which posits that racial oppression is, and has always been, a foundational piece of U.S. society. Today, that oppression continues to function in maintaining the unjust impoverishment and oppression of people of color, in contrast to the unjust enrichment of white Americans.[6] Systemic racism theory regards white supremacy as hegemonic and inescapable across time and region in the United States. Although some may point to the abolishment of enslavement, the civil rights era, and the twice-election of Barack Obama as proof that racial progress has occurred, systemic racism theorists understand that racism has merely changed form. Chattel slavery was replaced by formal segregation, which then evolved into mass incarceration, as well as more covert discriminatory segregation, laws, acts, and behaviors, including everyday racism.

To understand racism as systemic, we must let go of the fantasy that racism is only present when certain overt criteria are met. Of course, blatant anti-Black violence such as enslavement, lynchings, and racial slurs are understood by most to be racist. Many can even wrap their heads around mesolevel racism like police brutality, redlining, and the concentration of predatory lending in predominantly Black neighborhoods. Still, systemic racism theory asks us to think beyond individual racist events or phenomena and instead to recognize how not only action but also inaction and complicity at the micro and meso levels sustain white supremacy as an unrelenting macro social force.

For systemic racism to reproduce successfully and persistently, whites must be complicit in the system from which they benefit.[7] This complicity is fostered through the adoption of beliefs, actions, comments, and norms that legitimizes white domination and subsequently enacts both covert and overt anti-Black violence. Systemic racism theory points to an ideological framework that allows white supremacy to perpetuate this complicity over time: the white racial frame.[8] Those who adopt this dominant framework believe the preservation of racial inequality to be justified, through a combination of a white-is-right mentality, an adoption of controlling images of people of color, and an alleged color blindness that allows covert racism to go unchallenged.[9] The white racial frame paints whites as virtuous, well intentioned, and deserving of unearned enrichments, benefiting from symbolic racial capital while presuming race is an insignificant instrument in their successes. In turn, people of color—and specifically Black people—are painted through controlling images of being invisible, animalistic, uneducated, foreign, or dirty and, thus, *deserving* of a lower status in a racial hierarchy that is firmly controlled by whites.[10] However, I argue that intent is not a relevant tool of white supremacy in comparison to compliance and a refusal to name it. The microaggressions experienced by my respondents in the following chapters reflect exactly that: Regardless of intent, perpetrators of gendered racist microaggressions repeatedly demonstrated a common belief that whiteness was the golden standard, compared to which women of color are inferior, yet did so in such a way that accusations of racism could be denied.

Even though counterframes do exist to challenge this system, as the dominant framework in the United States, the white racial frame is so hegemonic that it continues to afflict even those who may not necessarily subscribe to its ideology.[11] Although white supremacy is considered a macro social force, it is not without the vested interest of individuals that it is upheld. White supremacy is contingent on anti-Blackness that allows race to operate in society as a hierarchy wherein white norms, ideologies, and practices are considered normal and favored. The adoption of these ideologies and practices at the micro level allows anti-Black violence, whether individual or structural, to become justified and unchallenged.

Perpetrators of microaggressions continue to uphold the racial hierarchy by disregarding the influence of systemic racism and by embracing the frameworks of white supremacy and one of its most utilized tools of maintenance: color-blind ideology. In his groundbreaking work, *Racism Without Racists: Color-Blind Racism and the Persistence of Racial Inequality in America*, sociologist Eduardo Bonilla-Silva notes four central tenets of color-blind racism that allow the disregarding of racism as a significant social force shaping everyday life: abstract liberalism, naturalization, cultural racism, and minimization of racism.[12] Each of these frames work collectively rather than individually to shape the way color-blind racism is used as an instrument of white supremacy. *Abstract liberalism* allows whites and others to disregard the centuries of formal and informal oppression that undoubtedly influence how race operates for people of color navigating today's society, instead relying on decontextualized bootstraps explanations for modern white dominance. This is also how law and policy that are seemingly race neutral continue to perpetuate anti-Black procedures. *Naturalization* and *cultural racism* use biological and cultural sweeping generalizations that allegedly confirm the logic and reasoning behind the cumulative effect of modern oppression. *Minimizing racism* is perhaps the most crucial behavior for microaggressive perpetrators to adopt, which rescues them from the label of racist by defining racism as solely overt, physically violent, and intentional by individual actors rather than as the contents of a cup from which we have all drank.

Color-blind ideology allows perpetrators to enact microaggressive comments or behaviors that justify anti-Blackness and buttress white supremacy, hidden behind innocuousness and weak rationale. By claiming they "do not see color," "do not see race as significant," or "have several friends of color," perpetrators can comfortably and successfully deny that their microaggression was racially charged at all and reject their subscription and dedication to upholding the white racial frame. Racist microaggressions depend on both color-blind ideology and systemic racism to exist. However, current research demonstrates how racist microaggressions change depending on other identities of the target and, as my research shows, the identities of the perpetrator as well.

Intersectionality and Critical Race Feminism

White supremacy in the United States does not fit neatly into any one box, as it overlaps, interacts, and collaborates with other social forces to retain its power and domination. Thus, white supremacy, anti-Blackness, and racism in general must be contextualized with its relationship to patriarchy, cisheterosexism, classism, and other forms of oppression that ensure both its adaptability and pervasiveness.

Beginning with Pierce's conception and continuing with scholarship that emerged in the 2000s following Sue's taxonomy, much of the microaggression discourse has emphasized a single marginalized identity: race, gender, sexuality, class, or ability. However, feminist scholars of intersectional theory argue that racism is never solely about race, and sexism is never solely about gender; rather, all of our identities, both privileged and marginalized, are situated within an intersecting structure within which our lives are shaped.[13] The inseparable reality of women of color's experiences with racism and sexism is denied when multiple oppressions are studied in discrete or additive ways. The experiences described by my respondents illustrate the ways in which white supremacy, patriarchy, and other macro-level oppressions like heterosexism and nationalism are intertwined throughout the microaggression experiences of Black and Asian American women, weaving a unique oppression that is, all at once, racialized, sexualized, *and* gendered, micro *and* macro, rather than either/or.

Indicative of the inseparable nature of identity and its relationship to power and oppression are controlling images. In her 1986 article, "Learning from the Outsider Within," sociologist and Black feminist Patricia Hill Collins introduced the concept of *controlling images*: stereotypes that justify and maintain the oppression of Black women.[14] This imagery is created by elite, powerful groups to make the oppression of Black women appear "natural, normal, and inevitable parts of everyday life" and are distributed through media such as film, TV, and advertising to infiltrate general perspectives.[15] By shifting the blame of social inequities onto those who are exploited by them, the outcomes of oppression and exploitation are cast as individual faults, and subscribing to controlling images to maintain white dominance becomes less outwardly apparent.

Expanded on in her book *Black Feminist Thought*, Collins provides examples of five controlling images that are projected onto Black women: the mammy, a faithful, obedient servant to white families; the matriarch, a bad Black mother who cannot model appropriate gendered behavior; the welfare mother (and subsequent welfare queen), a class-specific bad mother who may exploit public assistance for luxury items; and the Jezebel, a sexual deviant whose appetite for sex is insatiable.[16] Although these controlling images are labeled distinctly, they work in tandem to depict all Black women as poor, materialistic, uncivilized, lustful, and failed mothers—all qualities that are distanced from virtuous white womanhood. Feminist race scholars have expanded on Collins's work, identifying controlling imagery projected onto Asian American women and other women of color as well. Notably, the Lotus Blossom or China doll is a subservient, petite, tittering East Asian woman who exists to serve her white husband, and the Dragon Lady who is manipulative and power hungry and uses sex to manipulate trusting men. Seemingly at odds, these controlling images of Asian women are two sides of the same coin; they both cast Asian women as foreign objects to be conquered (whether via power or sex or both) by white men.[17]

Although the concept of controlling imagery has been extended to explore identities beyond that of Black womanhood, it is clear how they embody identities at the nexus of race, gender, sexuality, and class. As a component of maintaining white dominant ideology, the adoption of controlling images are on-the-ground attempts to justify the ills of white supremacist patriarchy, casting pervasive generalizations that exclude women of color—especially queer and/or poor women of color—from societal power and privileges.

Critical to situating the research for *Between Myths and Margins* intersectionally is acknowledging the interwoven facets of the matrix of domination, as conceptualized by Collins.[18] The matrix of domination embodies four interconnected domains, which contribute to sustaining white supremacist patriarchal social power over women of color. Each of these four domains rely on one another to create and maintain oppression at both macro and micro levels.

Within the matrix of domination, the *structural* domain of power organizes oppression in society through large-scale social institutions that subordinate women of color, such as polices, the U.S. legal system, the housing market, and education. When considered alongside Feagin's theory of systemic racism, the structural domain of power points to the ways in which white supremacy is more than simply the sum of individuals' racist behaviors. The *disciplinary* domain of power manages that oppression through organization, surveillance, and bureaucracy, ensuring the inequities appear fair and just on the surface. The *hegemonic* domain of power justifies oppressive actions through ideology, culture, and consciousness, normalizing systemic racism as an unspoken yet widely accepted tenet of U.S. society, consistent with Feagin's notion of the white racial frame and Bonilla-Silva's concept of cultural racism. These ideologies are dispersed through social institutions such as media, families, schools, and churches, casting women of color as personally responsible for their own systemic oppression. Last, the *interpersonal* domain of power functions through our daily, unremarkable practices: the systematic and routine thoughts and actions that perpetuate the subordination of women of color, emblematic of Essed's concept of everyday racism. Clearly, these domains are reflective of both micro and macro structures and their relationship to each other.

Intersectional theory has commonly been employed as a microlevel, individual concept, though this is a superficial use of the theory and discounts its history in Black feminism. The four domains of the matrix of domination serve to connect the micro, meso, and macro, the interpersonal to the systemic, as the crux of intersectional theory is, at its core, about power: the power of individual racialized bodies that form a collective group and collective responses, as well as the power of dominating systems. Collins distinguishes between *intersectional* and *interlocking*, claiming that interlocking describes social structures that create the social positions, while intersectional describes the location within that structure of oppression.[19] Accordingly, intersectional theory and method do not solely rely on examining the intersecting oppressions of individuals' identities per se but also (and primarily) on the ways that such identities are socially and historically created by interlocking systems of subordination as well.[20]

In agreement with both systemic racism theory and intersectional theory, this work is influenced by critical race feminist (CRF) perspectives as well. CRF, extended from critical race theory, posits that racism, sexism, classism, and other systems of oppression are endemic and structural in nature.[21] CRF specifically centralizes the experiences of women of color as the experts on their own marginalization, disrupting essentialism and instead suggesting that identities such as race, gender, sexuality, and class are inextricably linked.[22] CRF theorists perceive gendered racism as structural, present in laws, social policies, buildings, and other institutions that shape power and privilege in daily life. With this emphasis on structure, we can begin to understand microaggressions and everyday racism as tools of white supremacy, heterosexism, and patriarchy rather than as solely exchanges between individuals. This framework is indispensable when examining the interdependent nature of everyday racism and the macro social forces of white supremacist patriarchy.

Microaggressions Across Multiple Marginalities

Understanding gendered racism is imperative when examining microaggressions through an intersectional framework. Even though Philomena Essed did not use the term "microaggression" in theorizing everyday racism, her crucial work in *Understanding Everyday Racism* tied microlevel gendered, racist commonplace interactions to macro structures to explain quotidian racism and sexism as a by-product of institutional white supremacist patriarchism.[23] In her research interviewing Black women, she found that respondents would often share incidents of routine oppression they experienced, framed as frivolous injustices rather than major events. Although these experiences were described as specific incidents, Essed argues that each singular event recalls a cumulative instantiation as it evokes memories of other similar events and cognitive responses.[24] Everyday racism is not only about the event at hand but also the process by which such events sustain unequal power.

Racist microaggressions can and do change depending on respondents' gender, sexual orientation, ability, class, age, and religion and are not mutually exclusive.[25] Thus, racist microaggressions against women of color are always contingent on the position within a social hierarchy that one inhabits.[26] *Gendered racist microaggressions* are subtle behaviors, comments, or environmental slights that communicate oppression to the recipient, such as that they are lesser than, othered, or exoticized based on the intersection of their gender and race.[27] For example, Asian American women are largely exotified and fetishized by non-Asian counterparts and experience microaggressions that reflect this. However, this phenomenon is specific to Asian women; Asian men have historically faced entirely different hyposexualized or dangerous controlling imagery and accordingly experience quite different microaggressions than Asian women.[28] Similarly, Black women experience gendered racist microaggressions that perpetuate the controlling images of the *mammy* or the *welfare queen*, that differ from controlling images that portray Black men as violent criminals or gang members.[29] This contextualizes the variety of ways microaggressions are communicated and experienced. The addition of marginalized genders, sexual orientations, abilities, and religions only further alters the way microaggressions are perceived by both perpetrators and receivers alike.

Within the matrix of domination, Collins notes, "by manipulating ideology and culture, the hegemonic domain acts as a link between social institutions (structural domain), their organizational practices (disciplinary domain), and the level of everyday social interaction (interpersonal domain)."[30] Hegemony operates on the consensus that thoughts, feelings, and values of the oppressor are "common sense," creating a dominant framework that sets the standard for societal norms.[31] Microaggressions of all types are used to portray messages that anything outside of these commonsense beliefs is wrong, foreign, criminal, and deserving of exile. Patriarchy works concertedly with white supremacy to impose the superiority of what Audre Lorde referred to as the *mythical norm*: white, straight, young, masculine ideals, on all marginalized peoples, not solely limited to those of marginalized races.[32] For example, in the last decade, a spotlight on Black victims of police brutality has almost exclusively highlighted Black men, so much so that a social movement, #SayHerName, became necessary to acknowledge the many Black women who have suffered the same fate.[33] Whereas Tamir Rice, Michael Brown, and George Floyd are household names, Aiyana Stanley-Jones, Meagan Hockaday, and Mya Hall are not.

As a product of everyday racism, microaggressions operate to uphold the systemic nature of gendered racism. Feagin's theory allows us to understand racist behaviors as more than individual actions and beliefs, while Bonilla-Silva's contributions invite us to consider how racism has become invisibilized to protect its continued legacy. Collins's and CRF's extensive contributions further contextualize the influence of the white racial frame on media, our inseparable identities, and the importance of structural power, all evident in the microaggressions discussed by my respondents in the coming chapters. Although microaggressions have been primarily studied at the individual level, they are undeniably a tool of a system that allows individual racist interactions to permeate beyond the individual targets and perpetrators. Through a vested interest in maintaining white domination, perpetrators of white supremacist ideology utilize microaggressions that reflect color-blind racism, a subscription to controlling imagery, and buying into the meritocracy of power and subordination to maintain a racialized, gendered hierarchy that places women of color at the bottom rungs, all the while claiming progressive anti-racist politics as they insist their behaviors are not aligned with Racism-with-a-capital-R.

CHAPTER 3

Moving Toward Whiteness

Growing up, I knew very little of the Korean language. I could say basic childish phrases like, "I'm hungry," "Thank you," and "See you tomorrow." I could recognize the ten vowels and a handful of consonants of hangul (Korean), and I could use those characters to write my name: a two-syllable name suddenly became four, a German city that was never meant to be translated to a Korean tongue. My mother, having moved to the United States in her twenties, was bilingual. She sometimes spoke to us in hangul or asked her sisters to mail us Korean-language activity books, but learning to write or speak Korean fluently was never a priority in our home. On several occasions, I asked her why; the few other Korean kids I knew, mostly children of the Korean adults who rented the basement of a Presbyterian church after Sunday service, all spoke hangul to their parents. My mother's answer was always the same: "We didn't want you to get made fun of at school. We wanted you to speak *good English*."

My parents viewed *good English* as oppositional to speaking hangul: two mutually exclusive skills driving a choice of either/or. This attempt to protect my brother and me from racism was counterintuitive: despite being half-white, we are visually both racialized as Asian in the United States. We both still experienced racism from white classmates, but in addition, we experienced shame when other Koreans spoke to us in our mother's native tongue. My mother's push for us to be "American" enough to avoid racism came at the expense of appearing Korean at all; yet in any given space, we were only seen as either Korean or American.

Many first-generation children of immigrants in the United States have similar individual stories, yet it is important to consider the thread that binds our experiences to one another: the macro social influence of white supremacy. One of the most nefarious characteristics of white supremacy is how it permeates space.

Unsurprisingly, evidence suggests that people of color navigate nonwhite and white spaces differently and feel increased levels of anxiety and discomfort in spaces that are predominantly occupied by white people.[1] Still, macro social forces are defined by their hegemony; as much as we can attempt to insulate ourselves into enclosed bubbles of nonwhite spaces, ideologies shaped and maintained by white supremacy find ways to seep through any crack.

White racial framing permeates both white and nonwhite spaces, upholding beliefs and values that maintain racial inequality in similar ways as patriarchy, adopted and upheld in both male and nonmale spaces.[2] The interlocking nature of these two dominating frames culminates in a patriarchal white hegemony that values white men above all women and all people of color. The constant exposure to these interlocking ideologies, as well as the false guarantee that nonwhites will benefit from assimilation and subordination, leads many people of color to internalize and adopt their message. Consequently, messages in support of white patriarchal dominating ideologies are conveyed to Black and Asian American women by their families and peers of color through the use of gendered racist microaggressions.

Much of the existing microaggression research identifies perpetrators as those of a different race, gender, or sexuality than the receiver: even Pierce and Essed's foundational works describe whites as the executors of microaggressions and everyday racism.[3] Recent microaggression research also outlines several racial microaggressions specific to Black and Asian American people, including sexualization, being treated as second-class citizens, being perceived as perpetually foreign, and a pathologizing of cultural values and language.[4] Superficially, this focus on whites makes sense: Why would someone occupying the same or similar marginalized identities act in ways that oppress their companion along the same identity lines? However, throughout my conversations with Black and Asian American women, it became clear that many of their earliest experiences of gendered racist microaggressions came from within their own intraracial families and communities, including other Black and Asian American women. Black and Asian American respondents both shared incidents of their co-ethnic families and peers utilizing gendered racist microaggressions against them, regardless of the perpetrator's own race and/or gender identities that have been historically marginalized. Can we still classify these comments and behaviors as microaggressions when the perpetrators are also a people of color or even women of color? If the underlying message reaffirms whiteness as racially superior to nonwhiteness, then Pierce would likely argue yes.

Understanding the pervasiveness of the white racial frame as a tool of white supremacy contextualizes why women of color experienced gendered racism even when no men or white people were present. To be clear, I am not suggesting that people of color can be racist; this claim negates the facet of sociopolitical and economic power that is necessary for racism to truly exist. Instead, I argue that white supremacy and subsequent white racial framing are so omnipresent in U.S. society that even nonwhite people may internalize its poison, imposing these internalizations onto both themselves and others. We see evidence of this, for example, in an adoption and expectation of European beauty standards, colorism, texturism, and an insistence that white is right, even when no white people are in a given space. The following stories elucidate that Asian American and Black women are recipients of microaggressions inflicted from within their own racial groups, throughout both childhood and adulthood, as a consequence of white supremacist patriarchy.

The Desire for Whiteness

In developing his theory of systemic racism, sociologist Joe Feagin argues that the unjust enrichment of whites upholds white supremacy in the United States, both historically and in the present day.[5] This unjust enrichment includes power and privileges that, Feagin argues, are not earned through merit; rather, they are afforded to white people based solely on their whiteness. Although the alleged unmarked nature of whiteness may prohibit many people from recognizing these unearned privileges under the guise of meritocracy, people of color have borne witness to the advantages of whiteness in the United States for centuries.

These unjust enrichments shape the way whites continue to maintain power and privilege in the United States. On the surface, being racialized as white has allowed access to owning property, access to voting, and access to more comfortably resourced schools and public services; a deeper look into the powers of whiteness further exposes exclusively white access to healthier and longer lives, lower interest rates on housing and cars, the ability to create and dismiss laws, and the ability to break those laws with fewer consequences. Not surprisingly, those who are deprived of unearned enrichments can recognize from the margins that merit takes a back seat while whiteness is largely what determines success, access, and opportunity.

People of color are told, both overtly and covertly, that if we play by the rules—if we keep our heads down, if we don't play the race card, if we accept meritocracy as truth—we, too, can receive these advantages. But the full benefits of whiteness in America are not attainable for people of color—at least not unconditionally. Macro social forces like white supremacy operate in such a way that protects their domination from jeopardy; the rules are made by those in power and those rules keep the existing unequal racial structure in place. There's a reason the saying goes, "The house always wins." Still, the hope of one day obtaining those privileges—or even basic human rights—is dangled in front of nonwhites like a false promise, the goal posts constantly moving further back when neared.

Often, that false promise is enough to keep Black and Asian families desiring the power and privileges that whiteness affords. Throughout our interviews, Asian American and Black women shared accounts of their experiences in predominantly co-ethnic, nonwhite spaces. Some spent most of their time among peers and family that looked like them; others navigated both white and nonwhite space in equal measure due to their neighborhood, education or work institutions, or family structure. Many of these spaces were co-ethnic in which, for example, Korean Americans were in spaces occupied primarily by other Korean Americans, such as within a family; others were simply intraracial in which those Korean Americans were among other Asian Americans such as Chinese, Taiwanese, and Filipino Americans. Regardless of how much time they spent around other Asian and Black family and friends, they experienced gendered racist microaggressions that reflected a desire for some affiliation with whiteness, whether that was through assimilating to white cultural norms, through marriage to a white person, or through imitating white beauty standards.

In *Offensive Mechanisms*, Pierce provides five examples of microaggressive themes he has experienced, the last of which is "We whites are right."[6] He claims this theme is "the one from which springs all the others."[7] In this example, Pierce, a Harvard full professor at the time of his writing, describes incidents of white students who approach him after class to offer their opinions, from how his lectures should be structured to how the chairs should be arranged. Pierce acknowledges that these offerings are not discriminatory in principle; rather, he notes, "it is not what the student says in this dialogue, it is how he approaches me, how he talks to me, how he seems to regard me. . . . To him, I was nothing but a big black n—."[8] On the surface, the students' actions are mere suggestions to improve the class experience, but the underlying message communicated is that "whites know best." To Pierce, this inferred message shapes all other microaggressions, the purpose of which is to reassert the racial superiority of whiteness over Blackness.

In later microaggression research, psychologist Derald Wing Sue describes *pathologizing cultural values/communication styles* in his taxonomy of racial microaggressions.[9] I argue that pathologizing cultural values is contingent on the reinforcement of the social forces of white supremacy and white ideology as well as subsequent anti-Black ideologies, indicative of Pierce's original description of microaggressions as tools used to reinstate the superiority of whiteness. Today, generalizing aspects of white American culture are often the butt of jokes: from not rinsing their rice, to not washing their legs,[10] white Americans are not exempt from the pathologizing of "white cultural values." However, these jokes do not have the legacy of sociocultural domination that white supremacy does, and thus, although they are racialized, they do not carry the same social impact that true microaggressions do.

Systemic racism is a macrolevel system that acts on individuals and demonstrates the ways in which macro and micro are constantly in conversation with each other. Systemic racism creates alienation upon individuals between and within groups along racial lines. This alienation manifests through four social relations: (1) between whites and all people of color, (2) between separate races, such as Asian and Black Americans, (3) within a single race, and (4) within the self, actualizing as internalized racism.[11] In a society dominated by a white racial framework, assimilating to whiteness affords people of color *some* of the privileges of whiteness, without obtaining the structural power that whites possess through unjust enrichment. This strengthens the appeal for nonwhite families and nonwhite peers to pressure nonwhite women to desire, or aim for, symbolic whiteness, whether that is by affiliating with white friends and romantic partners, adopting certain ways of speaking, or engaging in white-dominated activities, without jeopardizing the systemic power that whites hold. When intraracial families and peers communicate to Asian American and Black women that assimilating or subscribing to white norms is preferable to Asian or Black norms through both macro- and microaggressions, white superiority and supremacy is further advanced within nonwhite communities. This cycle of macro influencing micro and, in turn, reinforcing the macro reflects the interdependent and cyclical nature of microinteractions (including microaggressions) and macro social forces.

The ways in which whiteness is pushed from within families and intraracial communities are distinct for women of color, as the expectation for marriage, beauty standards, and domesticity are not gender or race neutral. Thus, through the stories of my respondents, I identified *the desire for whiteness* as a gendered racist microaggression oft present in nonwhite spaces that are still influenced by white racial framing. The desire for whiteness manifests in different ways between the study respondents in two racial groups. Asian American families tended to encourage striving toward whiteness by prioritizing white romantic partners for their Asian American daughters, as well as communicating that assimilating to white cultural norms was superior to their own cultural norms. Black families' pressure to assimilate to whiteness was also espoused through pathologizing various Black cultural norms, as well as the message that typically white facial features, such as hair and skin tone, were superior. These differences must be considered in context of the unique, rich histories of colonialism, enslavement, and imperialism impacting Asian and Black migration to the United States.

The Prized White Man

The domination of white supremacy and patriarchy in the United States has led to white men and white masculinity holding the most societal power and influence. Respondents' Black and Asian family members communicated their desire to be adjacent to that whiteness and the societal power it imbues in several ways, whether it was pushing women of color to assimilate to it, prioritize it, or praise it as superior. This was especially common when it came to romantic partners. Asian parents in particular actively pushed respondents toward dating and marrying white men. Annie is a straight community organizer in her early twenties. With Taiwanese and Singaporean ancestry, she primarily claims Han Chinese ancestry. She was raised in a home where her mother was the primary earner, describing her household as "a strong-women household" consisting of herself, her older sister, her mother, and father. She describes the way her mother encouraged she and her sister to date white men in casual, day-to-day conversations:

> I remember my mom would point out white men as being the superior partner or, you know, maybe not saying exactly like that way but, you know, even she herself maybe expressing interest in them being better looking or having more means. . . . But I think that's something very vivid and interesting, if anything, with white men being seen as the superior partner to be with. My mom would also encourage me and my sister to not be with Chinese men in particular. Um, she thought, you know, she would raise us with very negative assumptions about Chinese men.

Even though Annie and her parents are Asian, her mother idealized white romantic partners for her and her sister, indicating that a white man was not only accepted but preferable to a Chinese man. Not only does Annie's mother discount Chinese men as good potential partners but actively disparages them to ensure Annie and her sister associated Chinese men with negative traits despite their own father—their mother's husband—being a Chinese man himself. For many Asian parents, white romantic partners were seen as the ideal sons-in-law and, in Annie's recollection, were also assumed to have wealth and success. The underlying message Annie and her sister received from their mother's comments communicated that white men were better looking, more successful, and ultimately better suited to be romantic partners than Chinese men. Thus, as a teenager, she felt pressure from her mother to date the prized white man.

What makes the white man "prized" to Asian mothers is reflective of a hegemonic white patriarchal supremacy, which places white masculinity as superior to other masculinities.[12] R. W. Connell describes hegemonic, marginalized, and subordinated masculinities as situated along a gendered and racialized hierarchy wherein hegemonic masculinity is associated with strength, logic, power, wealth, sexual virility, and whiteness.[13] Although few men truly embody every trait of hegemonic masculinity, sociologist Matthew Hughey claims that the average white male's gender socialization encourages white manhood to be "strong, autonomous, rational, neutral, objective." Hegemonic masculinity is simply off-limits to men of color.[14]

This is especially true for East Asian men, whose masculinity is often questioned and ridiculed within the white racial frame.[15] White standards of masculinity shape Asian American men as effeminate and asexual but also patriarchal, painting a contradictory picture of Asian American masculinity as both passive and dangerous. Recall the roles that Asian men have played in popular U.S. media for decades: from Sessue Hayakawa's depiction of the dangerous Hishuru Tori in *The Cheat* (1915), to Gene Watanabe's goofy Long Duk Dong in *Sixteen Candles* (1984), to Jacob Batalon's portrayal of sidekick Ned in *Spiderman: Homecoming* (2017). Until recently, male Asian characters have almost exclusively been depicted as dangerous, wacky, or nerdy but rarely relationship material. These contradictory images uphold racist tropes about the value of Asian men and their role in U.S. society; it's no surprise that the interlocking structures of white hegemony and patriarchy also shape mothers' perspectives on the ideal spouse for their daughters.

Further, Annie's mother demonstrates the expectation that Annie and her sister are both straight, pointing out white *men* specifically. In her study on Asian American sexual politics, sociologist Rosalind Chou found that Asian families communicated racial inferiority of romantic partners in subtle ways, but the expectation of heterosexuality was more overt.[16] This reflects the common adoption of compulsory heterosexuality in Asian households. Adrienne Rich describes *compulsory heterosexuality* as the blanket assumption that women are straight, erasing the lived experiences of lesbian women from feminist discourse.[17] Compulsory heterosexuality occurs not only within white America but in many cultures beyond the United States within which patriarchal ideology dominates. Each of my queer respondents, both Black and Asian American, discussed their parents' subscriptions to compulsory heterosexuality at some point in their lives.

Encouraging their daughters to date white men was an immensely common occurrence in Asian and Asian American households, regardless of ethnicity, and the message shaped many study respondents' perceptions of future partners.

Asian American women are more likely to marry outside of their ethnicity than any other race, and make up 75 percent of all Asian interracial marriages.[18] When Asian American women do marry outside of their own ethnicity, it is most often to white men than men of any other race.[19] Understanding the long-term implications of Western imperialism, colonialism, and Orientalism of Asian women gives context to these statistics, each of which cannot be disentangled from white supremacy.

Of fifteen Asian American study respondents, only three straight or bisexual women were coupled with Asian American men. Half of straight or bisexual Asian American women were coupled with white men, much to the approval of their parents. Consider Yuna, a straight, forty-year-old Korean American attorney, who grew up in the Virginia suburbs of Washington, D.C. Despite her parents moving to the United States in the early 1970s, their neighborhood was primarily occupied by Korean immigrants and businesses, allowing them to live in community with other Koreans. Still, Yuna grew up never fully learning hangul, the Korean language, which she describes as "intentional" on the part of her parents. "They wanted us to very much assimilate to American culture." Part of that American culture, to Yuna's parents, meant associating with white peers, classmates, and partners. Yuna describes the way her mother prioritized Yuna's white husband:

> I don't have children. I don't want to have children. And my mother, she's always afraid that people will think that my husband's mother especially hates me because I've been unable to give him a son. She's very much afraid of these ideas about like, her vocal fears that I failed his family because he's the only son, but I think her fear is, as an Asian woman, I failed a white man.

Yuna's mother implies two things through day-to-day, offhanded comments: that her white son-in-law will be disappointed in Yuna and that a male child would be the desired sex of a future child to carry on his family's name. The emphasis placed on not only having a child but a son exposes the dynamics of two ideologies adopted by Yuna's mother: the home-culture frame in which sons are highly preferred in Korean families, and the white racial frame in which Yuna's family should sanctify whiteness.[20] Although this message overtly suggests that Yuna may be disappointing her husband and his family, the shrouded implication is that both whiteness and maleness are the highest-ranking tier on a racialized gendered hierarchy and should be valued by individuals as such. Yuna's mom routinely conveys that major life decisions between Asian women and white men should ultimately result in the appeasement of the white male in the relationship, upholding white patriarchal hegemony.

The pressure to date white men by Asian parents does not exist in a vacuum; a preference for whiteness is rooted in anti-Blackness, a rampant issue that has been both acknowledged and ignored among Asian American communities and a consequence of systemic racism. White hegemonic patriarchy works to escalate internalized gendered racism within women of color, communicating that even one's own ethnic group is ranked below whiteness, while Blackness is rated at the lowest tier in a racial hierarchy. Even among the few Asian families that preferred respondents to date Asian men over whites, Black partners were entirely inconceivable. Asian American and Black respondents alike disclosed their parents' anti-Black sentiments while encouraging white men as romantic partners. Clara is a straight, half-Vietnamese, half-white woman, in her late twenties. She grew up in Georgia with her parents and older half brother where her family owned a nail salon that employed other Vietnamese workers. She described the way her Vietnamese mother reacted when she began dating a half-Black, half-white boyfriend in high school. She recalls:

CLARA: I think my parents have always preferred me to date white. So when I did date that one [guy] who was white and half Black, they were kind of shook. They're like, "Oh, that's weird." My mom . . . I don't know. She thought it was kind of gross, but I was like, well, that's kind of racist.

INTERVIEWER: Why did she say . . . why "gross"?

CLARA: I guess because she wanted me to date a white person. Yeah, I don't really know. It's really weird because in the nail industry, Vietnamese people talk so much shit about African American people. And African American customers. And even in Vietnam, it's like, they look down on them because of their skin color. And I'm like, what makes you better than them? Like, nothing does.

Clara receives her mother's message loud and clear: that white romantic partners are preferred, conveying her relationship is "gross" specifically because he is Black. While some families were critical of all interracial relationships, it was clear that her mother would find a relationship with a white man acceptable. Clara acknowledged her mother's distaste for her biracial boyfriend was discriminatory, but more specifically, it was rooted in anti-Blackness.

Clara further admits that her mother is only one of many Vietnamese people she interacts with that hold anti-Black sentiments while admiring whiteness. Many Asian immigrant parents had little interaction with Black people in their home countries and relied on controlling imagery that are portrayed through media to form schemas of Black communities. Controlling images of Black men and women alike paint them as poor, aggressive, and uneducated, ignoring the infinite variation of Black individuals and communities within the United States and beyond. These controlling images influence the perception of Black people in every role: as employees, friends, professionals, and romantic partners. A complex history of Asian immigrant-owned businesses operating in Black neighborhoods and violence between these groups further complicates Black-Asian community relations, driven by white supremacy.[21] This unrest can be traced back to controlling imagery of both Black and Asian peoples in the United States, wherein Asians are rendered the "good minority" in contrast to Black Americans as the "bad" ones. Of course, both stereotypes uphold essentialist ideology and white hegemony. Rather than acknowledging that both Asian and Black communities have been harmed by white supremacy within the U.S. borders and beyond, the adoption of a white racial frame and racialized controlling imagery ensures that marginalized groups remain in conflict with one another to prevent a coalition that could ultimately threaten the strength of white domination.[22]

Pressure from family members for respondents to date the prized white man was described by some Black women, though less so than among Asian American respondents. At the forefront to explain this difference is the understanding that anti-Blackness is severely gendered. Controlling imagery ensures Black women are cast as masculine, unfeminine, both hyper- and hyposexual, angry, and ultimately unmarriageable.[23] In contrast to white husband–Asian wife couplings, which have been shaped by decades of Western imperialism in Asia-Pacific countries, white husband–Black wife couplings are far less common at only 3 percent of all interracially married straight couples in the United States.[24]

Kala is a queer multiracial Guyanese woman in her late twenties who was raised in New York City. Growing up in a multigenerational household, Kala was surrounded by her large Dominican and Guyanese family with uncles, grandparents, and cousins all living on the same block. Most of her experiences with family pressuring her toward the prized white husband came from her mother, a Black Guyanese woman. Kala recognized the ways her mother policed her behavior and relationships through comments, actions, and setting rules that ultimately communicated her ideology that Blackness was inferior to whiteness. She recalls, "My mom told me when I was allowed to date, which was when I was, I think fourteen, and only because we had moved from Brooklyn to Westchester, which is predominantly white. That was my suburb; my school district was mostly whites. She said—and I quote—" I'd rather you be gay than come home with a Black man.' And I was like, "Wow, okay, so my mom is evil."

Kala believed she was only permitted to date once her mother perceived the risk of a Black romantic partner as unlikely due to the racial makeup of their new predominantly white neighborhood, and although this was not overtly stated, if there was any question about who Kala was expected to date, she made sure it was quite clear. Like Yuna's mother, Kala's mother situated white maleness at the top of a gendered racialized hierarchy even though her own husband, Kala's father, is a Black man. She further implicates queerness as only slightly more tolerable than Blackness. Even though Kala's mother's statement was quite blunt, it represents an everyday, routine message that she received throughout her childhood: that Black men—and all women—were not acceptable romantic partners; only white men will do.

Despite Kala's mother preferring that she date only white men, her romantic partners varied in race and gender prior to her marriage. Ultimately, Kala did marry a white man. Yet her mother continued to remind her that her own Blackness put the attainment of the prized white man at risk. At one point in our interview, she compared her mother to the painting *The Redemption of Ham* by Modesto Brocos, which features a dark-skinned Black grandmother praying in gratitude that her grandchild is white passing. She explains:

> I think that perfectly represents my mother, like she is so mired in her own internalized anti-Blackness and colorist issues that she is so excited that I have this white husband who affirms that I'm worthy. And so she will constantly, when I'm on FaceTime with her—I'm in Georgia, she's in New York—she'll see me outside in the sun and she'll be like, "Are you wearing sunblock? Go inside, you're gonna get too dark. What is Ben going to say? Don't get too dark for Ben, don't get *too Black*!" as if he will leave me at the slightest tan.

Kala's mother not only makes clear that white romantic partners are preferable but further ranks (what she perceives to be) the wishes of her husband Ben over her own nonwhite daughter's. She believes Ben will see Kala as unworthy of partnership, solely contingent on becoming too tan, or "*too Black!*," again perpetuating the message that Black skin is inferior to whiteness and that the attainment of white affection is as provisional as a summer tan. Pierce describes this internalized anti-Blackness as a delusion that cannot be changed even with hard evidence that contradicts Black inferiority: "Since Blacks have been victimized to sustain similar attitudes, all too often they too adopt pro-racist attitudes and behaviors in regard to themselves and to whites. Due to pro-racist attitudes in the United States, both Blacks and whites do things that permit, promote, encourage, sustain, and insist that whites are superior and Blacks inferior."[25]

In Name, In Food, Inferior

Given the macro nature of white supremacy, the term should be taken quite literally—the supremacy, dominance, and power, of whiteness. In the United

States, this must be contextualized within an understanding of how imperialism and colonization have shaped whiteness at the top of a racial hierarchy. Ruth Frankenberg reminds us that at the start of Europe's colonial project, identifying "cultures" and "peoples" was a strategy to separate Others from those in power to justify their colonization.[26] In the United States, this distinction allows whiteness to remain interwoven with "Americanness" in relation to culture and nationality as well. The supremacy of whiteness, then, ensures that cultural norms other than those dominated by white ideology remain subordinate.

Not only did Asian and Black families push respondents toward whiteness through a preference for prized white men, but they also implied that their own (nonwhite) cultural norms were lesser-than. This was evident in Annie's story as well as respondents like Eliza, a straight Filipina woman who shared that her mother cast Filipino men as unsuitable but white male partners as, literally, "the goal." In *Offensive Mechanisms*, Pierce provides the example "you Blacks are sick" to describe a microaggression that is utilized when whites want to display cultural power that reifies white supremacy.[27] This microaggression results in the target feeling uncertain of their lived experience: a racial gaslighting that situates a nonwhite experience as rooted in emotion rather than truth. The unchallenged nature of whiteness casts white cultural norms as neutral and standard, and any nonwhite cultural practices as *other* and, thus, inferior.[28] This message of white supremacy becomes reinforced through microaggressions. In later microaggression research, Sue describes *pathologizing cultural values* as microaggressions that suggest the values and language of the dominant culture are superior.[29] Although Sue specifically notes "values" and "communication styles" in his definition of this microaggression theme, I argue that this should be extended to encompass other cultural norms, including food, names, and holidays or customs that fail to center whiteness as truth.

As the white racial frame dominates U.S. ideology, it is not unreasonable for Asian families to subscribe to this presumption that whiteness *is* Americanness. For many Asian immigrant parents, encouraging their daughters to assimilate to whiteness, or Americanness, grants a false sense of comfort that their children will be protected from racism—just as my own mother thought when she did not prioritize teaching us Korean. Of course, regardless of how "Asian" or "white" my respondents seemed to their co-ethnic communities, anti-Asian microaggressions that reinforce white superiority were ever present.

The glorification of whiteness was imparted on Asian American women through familial pressures to conform to American (white) culture, including language, food, and even names. Consider Lizzie, a queer Korean American social worker in her twenties. Lizzie immigrated to the United States from Korea with her parents and younger brother in the late 1990s. For the first year or so, she went by her Korean-origin name as she adjusted to life in a new country. She describes teachers and peers constantly asking if she had a nickname because her name was "too hard to pronounce." Eventually, Lizzie changed her Korean-origin name to a classically American-sounding name at the advice of her parents. She shares:

> My name is Lizzie. I picked it when I was six or seven. It's such a funny story now. I used to watch this show called *Lizzie McGuire*; there's this character Lizzie. She's like, white and blond and really smart. So I named myself after her. I wanted to be white, I want to have blond hair and be pretty and to be characterized as the pretty girl. So I picked my name after her. I didn't even realize it. I told that story all the time and didn't realize how messed up it was until I was a full-grown adult. My brother did the same thing! He went by Matthew [Lizzie's brother in the TV show]. And now I'm legally changing my name to Lizzie because it's just become so convenient.

Lizzie McGuire was a Disney Channel TV series that aired from 2001 to 2004, the same period that my respondent moved to the United States from Korea.[30] The titular character, played by Hilary Duff, is a middle school–aged, all-American teen navigating life with her two best friends, younger brother Matthew, and straight, white, middle-class parents. Episodes revolve around her interacting with her longtime crush, navigating the school bully, and picking the right outfit for her school's yearbook photos. All in all, *Lizzie McGuire* embodies what it means to be a white, middle-class girl living in the United States.

As a child, study respondent Lizzie associated Americanness with whiteness and chose a name that she believed embodied the epitome of whiteness: a name that, to her, suggests conventionally white features of blond hair and light-colored eyes, as Hilary Duff possessed. Rather than encouraging her to embrace her given name in a new country, Lizzie's parents imply that Americanness (and by association, whiteness) should be adopted over Korean norms in attempts to appear assimilated.

Pathologizing cultural norms such as names and food was persistent within the families of Asian American women. These microaggressions communicate to Asian American girls and women that Americanness, by way of whiteness, is celebrated and strived for, while Asianness is to be forgotten, hidden, or shamed. This message was perpetuated by Asian parents to reflect even seemingly insignificant norms of Asian households. Yuna shared that her mother rarely allowed her friends to visit their home when she was growing up in a suburb of Washington, D.C. Her mother believed their home was not Americanized enough to expose it to non-Korean guests. Yuna recalls, "I just didn't have a lot of Asian friends growing up. Maybe that would have made the difference, but she was very much afraid of being judged. By anybody. She thought the house was messy or that it smelled like kimchi or that it smelled like an Asian house, and I was like, I don't even know what that means! [laughs] I was like, isn't our house just a house?"

Yuna's mother thought the smell of a Korean family's food and home was something to be ashamed of in the United States; something that should not be shared with non-Korean guests for fear of judgment. On the few occasions Yuna's friends did visit their family home, her mother would cook meals of scrambled eggs, spaghetti, and hot dogs, rather than the Korean dishes she usually cooked for her family. Instead of portraying an assimilated American family, this random mishmash of breakfast and dinner foods in a single meal only further depicted Yuna's family as "forever foreign" to outsiders.

Although it may seem like an endearing attempt to ensure Yuna's friends felt welcomed as guests in their home, Yuna's memory of the occasions is shrouded in frantic chaos and fear of judgment. Asian immigrants are promised that greater assimilation to U.S. norms and culture will grant their children the benefits and privileges of whiteness. Any lingering customs—whether food, language, religion, or style—otherizes Asian immigrants as foreigners. Years later, Yuna is able to rebuff some of her parents' implications that being Korean was inferior to whiteness and Americanness. However, many other Asian American respondents adopted this message into adulthood. Take Annie, whose mother demonstrated a desire for her to date the prized white man. Annie notes how these slight messages of white superiority influenced her relationships with her peers. Her mother's glorification of whiteness socialized Annie from a young age to perceive other Asian Americans negatively, even beyond a preference of white romantic partners:

> I think my mom's discouragement of, you know, getting together romantically with Han Chinese people affected my friendships as well because I went to Chinese school on Saturdays for a good amount of my life and I remember being really annoyed with the people I had to be with. I was like, intentionally being bad at Chinese there, because I was so annoyed at how good at Chinese they were; thinking they were obnoxious or, you know, socialized to believe that. And I think that carried on through middle school and high school; I didn't have, for instance, a lot of Korean American friends.

In adulthood, Annie identifies her mother's desire for a white partner as a product of white supremacist ideologies, but as a child, she tried to distance herself from other Asian Americans by sabotaging her grades in Chinese school and solely socializing with non-Asian peers despite growing up with many Asian American classmates. By intentionally performing poorly in Chinese school, Annie illustrates the internalization of her mother's message that Chinese culture is inferior to whiteness. Annie's mother illustrates a common contradiction within Asian American families: Annie and her sister were sent to weekend Chinese school to learn about cultural values, language, and norms, yet her mother also disparaged Asian men as suitable romantic partners and hoped her daughters would marry into white families. This left Annie with a dissonance regarding whether Chinese values were worthy of upholding in lieu of white Americana.

If Not Whiteness, Lightness

Although not discussed explicitly in Pierce's early microaggression literature, colorist microaggressions reflect an ideology that implies the superiority of whiteness. J. Camille Hall and Jandel Crutchfield identified colorist comments as fitting the definition of microaggressions that centralize white standards of beauty.[31] Colorist microaggressions may subtly communicate to Black and brown women that lighter complexions—and those that appear closer to white skin—are the most desirable, beautiful, and worthy. They occur both within and outside of Black and brown communities and thus have become a crisis even in communities that are not proximate to whiteness.[32] Subsequent microaggressions communicate that darker skin on women and girls of color is something to be ashamed of and corrected, often through dangerous skin lightening products.

Colorist microaggressions from families and co-ethnic communities were common in most Black women study respondents' experiences, regardless of the tone of their complexion; even lighter skinned Black women reported incidents of colorist microaggressions they had experienced from other Black women. Colorism occurs as a by-product of alienation from within racial groups, caused by systemic racism.[33] Again, white supremacy cannot be disentangled from colonialism and imperialism. Frantz Fanon notes that enslaved African Americans were first alienated from African cultures by the adoption of the English language; subsequent forced abandonment of culture and adoption of dominant (white) group practices have since transformed to a preference for lighter skin, which symbolizes the truth, purity, and power of whiteness.[34]

Importantly, colorism is extremely gendered in nature. Black and brown women are more likely to suffer from life-altering circumstances because of their complexion than Black and brown men. Alienation within a racial group occurs across gendered lines, but alienation by way of colorism is particularly significant in the lives of Black and brown women. Researchers have found a double standard in which darker skin on Black male romantic partners is preferred by Black women partners.[35] In contrast, dark skin on Black women impacts them economically, psychologically, and sociopolitically, as light complexions on women and girls in particular is understood as superior.[36]

Sadly, colorist microaggressions that imply the superiority of lightness and whiteness occur at remarkably young ages for Black girls and women. Briana is a thirty-two-year-old queer Black mother living in rural Georgia while working on her PhD. She chose an apartment near her own mother's house so that she could have familial help caring for her toddler. Although Briana and her mother are both a deep brown in complexion, she recalls the way her mother criticized darker skin when Briana's daughter was born:

> With my baby, when she was first born, she was, I don't know if you've seen pictures, but she was darker than she is now. . . . And her ears were like, *black*, and I remember my mom *hating* when people would say like, "Oh, she's such a—" people call her Chocolate Chip or, you know, saying, "She's such a beautiful dark baby" and all these different things, calling her dark chocolate. And she was like, "Well, she's not *that* dark" and I'm thinking to myself, "Well, Mom, she is. And it's okay. And the only comment that's making me upset right now is you, by not acknowledging how dark she is as if it's a bad thing."

By insisting that her granddaughter was "not *that* dark," Briana's mother inflicts a colorist microaggression that ascertains darkness is undesirable and unattractive. Briana does not take offense to the nicknames that others have given her daughter that describe her dark complexion; rather, she recognizes that her mother's distaste for dark skin is rooted in a preference for light skin—a preference that is contingent on desirable features and their proximity to whiteness.

Perpetrators' own Blackness is perhaps what makes colorist microaggressions so dangerous for Black women: the way microaggressions can typically be explained away by a white perpetrator (i.e., *I'm not racist; I have Black friends!*) is amplified when the inciter is a member of the same racial background as the respondent.[37] Colorism is rooted in anti-Black sentiments that further uphold white patriarchal supremacy by ranking skin tone on a continuum of light to dark for women of color. Darkness can only be attributed to negativity inasmuch as lightness is attributed to positivity. There exists a long prevalence of black and white dualism throughout religion, history, and pop culture that defines darkness as undesirable in juxtapose to the desirability of lightness. Thus, it is only through a guarded maintenance of white supremacy that anti-Black sentiments flourish, even within Black families and communities. Such preferences within communities of color point to the strength of a penetrative white racial frame.

Pathologizing dark skin has been rampant in media, the criminal justice system, education, employment, and both physical and mental health services.[38] Although pop culture and media have increased Black representation in recent years, lighter complexions take priority, with outlets even photoshopping existing dark skin to appear lighter. Seeing these images in everyday life establishes to Black and brown girls what is considered beautiful and even worthy. Sailem is a Black college student in her early twenties who moved to Atlanta from rural Georgia. She grew up surrounded by extended family including grandparents, aunts, and cousins whom she describes as all "on the spectrum" of light to darkness in skin tone. The variance in skin color (and the supposed value behind it) was a sensitive, yet often discussed, subject among her family members. She recalls an incident where her cousin associated lighter skin with achievement and success:

> SAILEM: She's fucking pretty. The bitch is just fucking pretty, okay. She should have been a model. I don't know what she's doing, but she's short. She's my height, so put on some heels and get up there! Her face is so freaking symmetrical you know, it's crazy. But she's the darkest one out of her sisters. And Priscilla is the lightest one, so she's yellow, you know, yellow (laughs). And so when they were talking, she said—and I quote—"Yeah, I deserve to be light skinned."
>
> INTERVIEWER: [pause] What does that mean?
>
> SAILEM: It means exactly what you think it means. Yeah, like "I'm too pretty to be dark skinned. I deserve to be light skinned."
>
> INTERVIEWER: What did [the other cousins] say?
>
> SAILEM: They laughed and I looked at her. I really looked at her and I'm like, "Girl, you're *what*? What the fuck are you talking about? Your mom is dark skinned; your dad is dark brown. Girl, you're gorgeous, you *deserve* to be light skinned? Where are you getting this?"

The shame Sailem's cousin felt regarding her skin tone is contingent on the way she witnesses society's judgment of dark skin; it's no surprise Sailem's cousin internalized anti-darkness messages. Here, the concept of deserving is especially damaging, as if the benefits of whiteness are something that can be earned through playing the right cards. She saw lighter skin as a prize to be won by someone deserving of its privileges rather than a complexion randomly attributed to genetics and perhaps luck. By commenting that she was deserving of lighter skin to her deep brown sisters and cousin, she reaffirms anti-Black violence to her family, implying their own dark skin, and all the societal consequences of having dark skin, is not deserving of admiration. The underlying message is, once again, that adjacency to whiteness is superior and that dark-skinned girls will never be as beautiful—or deserving—as light-skinned girls.

Zenia, a queer Black nineteen-year-old college student, also shared the microaggressions she received that light skin was superior to dark skin. Having grown up in a predominantly Black area, her daily life consisted of Black teachers, schoolmates, neighbors, and friends as well as Black media. She recalls noticing colorist microaggressive comments more so than general anti-Blackness. "There would be subtle messages in media, from my classmates, that light-skinned girls were better. So you know, growing up with *Martin*, all these shows with dark-skinned girls as hoochie mamas, or she is angry." Not only was Zenia subjected to the glorification of light skin within Black communities and media, but she also saw how dark-skinned women were more often portrayed as the controlling image of the Angry Black Woman, reinforcing that Black woman, and especially those without some white lineage, are unreasonable, angry, and loud.[39] Zenia noticed the ways in which media characterized Angry Black Women tropes as deliberately dark skinned, further marginalizing dark Black women through this controlling image more so than the marginalization of their gender and race alone.

When colorist ideologies are constantly supported on TV shows, in music, and even through family comments and behaviors in predominantly Black spaces, resisting the internalization of those messages can take an emotional and psychological toll on Black women. Vanesia is a Nigerian American college student whose mother immigrated to the United States from Nigeria. At the time of our interview, she was living with her mother in a predominantly white suburb of Atlanta and commuted into the city to attend college classes. Vanesia notes her mother's colorism was consistent and unyielding throughout her childhood. She shared that her mother would give her skin-lightening creams and soaps under the guise of a casual gift, without telling her their actual intended purpose. Even though Vanesia recognized and worked to resist the anti-Black messages of her mother's microaggressions, she still found herself internalizing colorist beliefs about her own dark skin as well as other Black women's:

> VANESIA: There was always a tension for me not feeling fully comfortable in my skin because my mom obviously thought lightness was better and I did experience racism and colorism in my day-to-day life, so I wished I could go ahead and go for the leap and lighten my skin, or that it would just be taken out of my hands so I would stop having to feel that internal conflict.
>
> INTERVIEWER: Have you embraced your dark color?
>
> VANESIA: It's still a day-to-day process for me because I still live with my mom and she's still toxic. But it's because I can see on other people, I see them and

> I'm like, um, you should be a couple shades lighter. So it's psychosis! If I can see them and embrace them for what they are, I have to be able to do that for myself, and it's still kind of difficult.

Skin-bleaching and hair-straightening practices indicate the internalization of racialized and colonial notions of European beauty aesthetics. These standards are rooted in gendered, racialized, and sexualized social meanings that are created and shaped by whites to maintain white supremacy and to police respectability and identity politics among people of color.[40] Although all women are subjected to unrealistic standards of beauty shaped by patriarchy, women of color are expected to conform to both racial domination and gender domination simultaneously.[41] Until white supremacy is dismantled, individual rejection of these ideologies may take intentional and purposeful learning, as colorist messages are frequently enforced through both microaggressions and more blatant means. Actively unlearning these ideologies proved difficult for Vanesia, who received multiple colorist microaggressions in the predominantly Black spaces she frequented. For example, when her Black peers ridiculed her dark complexion by nicknaming her "Charcoal," she felt powerless to escape these relentless messages as they permeated both her home and school life. She was unable to find support from other dark Black girls and thus felt isolated within a community that subscribed to uphold white standards of beauty. "It was really terrible to work through on my own. I couldn't talk to my mom about being called Charcoal because then she might be like, 'oh, just lighten your skin to solve these problems!'" Vanesia's struggle between wanting to feel comfortable in her own skin and receiving messages that her skin was not beautiful from both peers and family reflects the heartbreaking ways in which incessant colorist microaggressions may impact the self-worth of Black women.

Conclusion

Intraracial family and peers microaggressed Black and Asian women through everyday racist comments and behaviors that indicated a desire to be proximate to whiteness in some way. Whether through an indication of acceptable romantic partners, pressure to assimilate to white cultural norms, shaming of their own heritage culture, or disdain for dark skin, my respondents' time spent in nonwhite spaces was still infiltrated with white supremacist ideologies that uphold a gendered racist hierarchy where white men reign unchallenged. White patriarchal supremacy is so normalized, so routine that its influence challenges the potential of coalitions between and within nonwhite communities to dismantle it. As George

Lipsitz writes, "the power of whiteness depended not only on white hegemony over separate racialized groups, but also on manipulating racial outsiders to fight against one another, to compete for white approval, and to seek the rewards and privileges of whiteness for themselves."[42]

While conducting this research, I struggled to name this particular theme; it was clear that the root of these microaggressions was, as Pierce surmised, the message that whiteness is superior to racialized Others. However, seeing that message come from the mouths of communities of color was difficult. If other families of color are like my own, I imagine few would outright forfeit their own identities, cultures, and realities to adopt whiteness in full if given the opportunity despite the constant exposure to anti-Asian and anti-Black everyday racism. Clearly, there are many accounts of parents and peers who want to preserve their cultural practices, yet who also perpetuate microaggressions that communicate those same tenets of daily life are inferior to white ones. Important to consider here is the agency involved in respondents and their communities moving toward whiteness. Whiteness is, after all, the standard and norm by which we are all measured. Assimilating to whiteness often means being afforded privileges that Black and Asian Americans are not otherwise privy to, and those privileges may very well be related to psychological and physical safety. There is a personal negotiation in the move toward whiteness; we can choose to straighten our hair, use skin-lightening creams, perfect dialects, and code switch to play the part of the perfect American citizen if it means we get closer to the dream job, the desired spouse, or even get home safely after a police encounter. Possessing a double consciousness allows nonwhites to understand their racial positioning and to make informed choices based on the flexibility (or instability) of that position. Yet, that agency is calculated against the risk of what it may mean to stay outside of the dominant framework of whiteness.

Rather than an indication that communities of color want to *be* white, I argue this phenomenon is a product of nonwhite communities understanding quite clearly the unearned benefits that whiteness affords. As much as whiteness is perceived as unraced or unmarked, it is certainly not invisible from the margins. All things considered, my respondents' stories brought me to realize that for communities of color, the desire for proximation to whiteness is often not explicitly about whiteness itself but about the desire to be seen as worthy of humanity.

CHAPTER 4

The Right and Wrong Kind

Social scientists and genetic biologists alike understand race is not biological; rather, it is constructed and upheld by societal interpretation.[1] Classifications of race and the racialization of people are contingent on both time and location. Critical race theorists argue that in the United States, these classifications have largely been contingent on law.[2] Consider the Supreme Court cases *Ozawa vs. United States* (1922) and *United States v. Bhagat Singh Thind* (1923) that demonstrate the instability of racial categories. *Ozawa* ruled that Asians, regardless of years spent living and working in the United States, were not eligible for naturalized citizenship under the Naturalization Act of 1906. This ruling was contingent on the argument that they were not "Caucasian"—descendants of the Caucasus Mountains—the court's criteria for whiteness.[3] Following *Ozawa*, Thind, an Indian Sikh man, petitioned for, and was granted, naturalized citizenship in the United States due to his Aryan-Indian ancestry of which he argued was indicative of lineage from the Caucasus Mountains. In response, government attorneys proceeded to rescind his newly granted citizenship shortly after. Just three months following the *Ozawa* ruling, Thind argued that he was legally white based on the court's definition of "free white persons" being descendants of the Caucasus Mountains and thus entitled to the naturalized citizenship. The Supreme Court once again shifted the definition of whiteness to solely accommodate European whiteness, reclassifying Caucasian ancestry as it is "popularly understood" rather than its literal definition, of which includes many people with both Asian and European heritage.[4] Within a matter of months, the definitions of whiteness had shifted.

Even within a single decade, classifications of race have differed depending on individual states' legislation. The year following *Thind*, the Virginia General

Assembly enacted the Racial Integrity Act in which interracial marriage was banned and whiteness was classified as a person with "no trace of the blood of another race."[5] Multiple state legislations across the United States, including in Florida, Tennessee, Maryland, and Utah, have ruled that persons with one-eighth, one-sixteenth, one-thirty-second, or the vaguely defined "one drop" of nonwhite ancestry were classified as entirely nonwhite (and thus denied many of the formal benefits of whiteness despite visually reading as white in many cases).[6] Pierce would classify these laws as macroaggressions, and they are but few examples of the many ways race classification in the United States has been shaped by law, has been fragile and manipulable, and has shifted definitions when necessary to preserve white hegemony. Underlying each of these cases is the dominant white ideology that shapes U.S. law, calling the shots on who is deserving of the benefits of whiteness and who is not.

The notion that one can be more or less of their own racial identity is rooted in a globalized white ideology in which racialized peoples are measured against dominant whiteness. For African and Asian diaspora, this is further reinforced by *forever foreign* controlling imagery in which all Asian and some Black peoples in the United States are perceived as recent immigrants. As with all controlling imagery, the standard of what is and is not American is defined by white hegemony. Because whiteness is conflated with Americanness in the United States, Asian and Black Americans who participate in American norms are often seen by their co-ethnic family and peers as *too Americanized* (white) or distanced from their motherland or culture. The boundary between assimilating to American norms while simultaneously upholding exclusively nonwhite cultural values and norms is an unattainable obstacle for Black and Asian American women.

Counter to receiving microaggressions that communicated whiteness is superior, Black and Asian American study respondents' own families and intraracial communities engaged in comments that implied respondents were not Black or Asian "enough." In other words, they understood the message that they were the wrong *kind* of Black or Asian. These messages were received by both Black and Asian women, more often from peers than from family members. Marc Johnston and Kevin Nadal situate many of these behaviors within multiracial microaggressions, under several themes including *exclusion or isolation* and *denial of multiracial reality*.[7] They describe these microaggressions as occurring when a multiracial person is excluded due to their multiracial status or when they are denied the opportunity to choose their own racial identity. My multiracial respondents did share instances of microaggressions fitting into these themes. However, I argue that a behavior or slight that conveys someone is not a true member of their race falls within Pierce's examples of microaggressions for full-Black and -Asian

American women as well rather than as exclusive to multiracial groups. This became evident as many of my respondents who identify as fully Black or fully Asian (rather than mixed race) shared instances of exclusion and justification of their racial identities within nonwhite spaces.

On the surface, this microaggressive theme may seem to clash with the desire for whiteness or white adjacency; however, they share an underlying foundation when considering the relationship between macro and micro dimensions of gendered racism. Individualism is deeply entrenched within the structure of white supremacy; the ability to be viewed as an individual, and thus for racist actions to be seen as a product of individual rather than group decisions and beliefs, allows individuals to avoid accountability for systemic and collective racism that whites themselves benefit from.[8] Individualism is a privilege afforded to whites, who view themselves and other whites as "unraced" or "race neutral" rather than as racialized at all. In contrast, people of color are rarely afforded the privilege of individualism, instead viewed as parts of a group sum representative of their race. Controlling imagery of women of color furthers the ideology that there is a standard by which they behave that confirms their membership to a racialized group.

The contention that Asian American and Black women must engage in a set standard of behaviors, clothing, tastes in music, or types of hobbies in order to be a "real" member of their race or ethnicity discounts the complexities of people racialized as nonwhite and casts women of color as monolithic. The standard of acceptable activities and behaviors for Black and Asian women are rooted in the controlling images within each race. Controlling images paint "real" Asian women as docile and unacculturated to U.S. customs and cast "real" Black women as hypersexual, angry, and uneducated. Through an internalization of these stereotypes and an adoption of white racial framing, Asian and Black communities microaggressed study respondents by implying they did not belong within their self-identifying racial category.

Language as Membership

The ability to speak a language fluently acts as a social marker for who has assimilated and who has not, drawing boundaries around who is perceived as belonging in the United States. For many Asian Americans, speaking English exclusively or better than a heritage language implies a proximity to whiteness that non-native English speakers are not afforded. Speaking English alone is not enough; it must be spoken without an accent that indicates it was learned outside of U.S. borders. For Asian Americans who hope to distance themselves from their ancestral heritage, speaking English well is a source of pride: an indication that one truly belongs in the United States.[9] However, that indication of membership goes both ways; Asian Americans who learned English as their first, and perhaps only, language may appear *too* Americanized to those who learned English as a second language.

Nari is a queer Korean American woman in her mid-twenties. She was born and raised in a predominantly white town in Georgia by Korean immigrant parents. When Nari was fourteen, she noticed an influx of Korean immigrant families moving to her town and attending her public school. Although she speaks Korean fluently, she did not become close with these students. "Because I was born and raised here, they just saw me as a very white person."

As previously described, the tendency to associate whiteness with Americanness is not unusual for immigrant Asian families. Race in the United States is typically framed in terms of whiteness and Blackness, so it is not surprising that Nari's Korean classmates discounted her Asian *American* experiences as *white* experiences.[10] Nari recounted incidents of microaggressions at the hands of her Korean peers who associated all U.S.-raised Asian Americans with white lived experiences. These assumptions of white adjacency conveyed to Nari that, to her Korean peers, she was *not Korean enough*.

During their individual interviews, both Nari and her partner, Lizzie, also Korean American, shared that within Asian American communities, there are terms used to distinguish between immigrant Asians and those who were born and raised in the United States: FOB (fresh off the boat) and ABC (American-born Chinese). These terms serve as symbolic social boundaries that maintain a distinction between Asian peers dependent on how assimilated to American culture they are.[11] The term "FOB" refers to immigrants of Asian descent who migrated to the United States but have not assimilated to U.S. cultural norms, language, or traditions. FOB is largely considered a derogatory term, though Karen Pyke and Tran Dang found it is used most often within Asian ethnic communities rather than by non-Asians.[12] On the other hand, ABC is used to describe Asian Americans who maintain very few of their heritage's cultural norms. They may only speak English, eat mostly American foods, and have primarily non-Asian or other ABC friends. Although ABC specifically refers to Chinese ethnic groups, it has been adopted and applied to other Asian ethnicities who are U.S. born or raised. Both terms reflect controlling images and monolithic assumptions imposed on Asian American communities. The FOB clearly mimics the forever-foreign stereotype of Asians who are unwilling or incapable of assimilating to Americanized (white) culture—they are, as the name implies, freshly immigrated. In contrast, the ABC represents a submission to white cultural norms and willingness to be dominated by other forms of whiteness. Although Nari's casual use of both terms suggest she had internalized these controlling images herself, she claims she did try to befriend the Korean immigrant students in her classes:

> I remember being friends with them but not really being friends. They spoke Korean in front of me thinking that I wouldn't understand Korean. I got, I don't want to say bullied, it's not bullied, but I remember in class these Korean people were talking about me blatantly. "*Nuguya? Megook saram gotche saeng gyeoseo?*" They used to say stuff like that, which is essentially, "Who is this girl? She isn't Korean; she's American. She doesn't speak Korean." I turned over [laughs] . . . I turned over just to hear. They took advantage of the language barrier we had. It made me feel like shit.

Nari speaks and understands enough Korean to know what her classmates were saying about her. Still, she felt so humiliated by this experience that she asked her parents to enroll her in Korean-language classes to become better familiarized with her heritage. Although she felt bullied by other Korean students at the time, as an adult, she recognized that their ostracism of her was a form of their own self-protection. She witnessed incidents of other U.S.-born students, both Asian and not, mocking the Korean immigrant students' English and that as an "ABC," she was perceived as the bullies' associate. Nari continues, "They knew that I personify ridicule in a sense: me coming to them, trying to make friends with them, knowing that it's not possible. . . . They were kind of like, 'Are you trying to make fun of us? Because you're trying to *be* us, but you're *not* us.' It's like, you don't want to be them, but you *are* them."

Reflected here is the dilemma that many Asian Americans reportedly face in the United States: the assumption that *Asian* and *American* are two mutually exclusive categories of which one can hold membership. As W. E. B. Du Bois described the *double consciousness* experienced by Black Americans, Asian Americans, too, are tasked with viewing themselves as they are perceived by others—not only by whites but also by other Asians.[13] Experiencing a double consciousness undermines one's identity—Nari finds it difficult to navigate the world as a U.S.-born Korean American while others treat her as exclusively American or exclusively foreign. To her classmates, she cannot be both Korean *and* American, cannot truly befriend them while also assimilating to those who belittle them. To differentiate themselves from Nari and other ABCs, her Korean immigrant classmates would quiz her about how often she ate Korean food and whether she could speak Korean with a *Seoulmal* dialect.[14] These arbitrary tests conveyed that Nari was too Americanized to claim a Korean identity and that, from their perspectives, she benefited from the subsequent privileges of American whiteness. However, many microaggressions reportedly experienced by Asian international students have also been experienced by U.S.-born Asian Americans.[15] Despite being viewed as an ABC by other Koreans, Nari was not protected from forever-foreign controlling imagery at all.

Language was often a defining factor in whether my Asian American respondents received microaggressive messages that they were not the "right kind" of Asian. Lizzie grew up in Kentucky and had similar experiences of ostracism from Korean immigrant students because she did not speak Korean well despite having been born in Korea. Sarah, a multiracial Chinese, Korean, and white thirty-one-year-old, felt she was not welcome at her university's Chinese American Affinity Group because she could only speak English. Charlotte, a queer Japanese and Taiwanese woman in her late twenties, admitted she did not even attempt to join an Asian American college student organization for the same reason.

Similar to Asian American women who were excluded from Asian spaces based on the inability to speak heritage languages, Black women's Blackness was challenged based on their dialect and language use. Language served as an indicator of how legitimate their Blackness was perceived by co-ethnic peers. Andrea is a thirty-two-year-old queer Black woman who was raised in a predominantly Black town in southwest Georgia. Many of her classmates spoke in African American Vernacular English (AAVE), paired with a Southern U.S. accent. Andrea, however, did not use AAVE or speak with an apparent Southern accent. As a middle schooler, she received microaggressive messages from her classmates that implied *real* Black people spoke in a specific way: "I remember comments because of how I talked, which is without an accent essentially, without a Southern accent. And without African American vernacular. Comments like 'You talk white,' or 'You sound white,' or 'You want to *be* white.'"

Andrea's classmates associated her dialect with whiteness, reinforcing the message that Blackness is contingent on exemplifying controlling images. Not only was she accused of "sounding white" but also of wanting to *become* white because of the way she spoke. These accusations draw distinctive racialized boundaries around language and behaviors. The microaggressions Andrea received specifically accused her of subscribing to and striving toward whiteness; and while the prior chapter illuminated an intraracial expectation for women of color to strive toward whiteness, respondents were also criticized for the very same. The contradiction places women of color in an impossible location.

The relationship between gendered racist microaggressions, academic achievement, and dialect is clear when examining controlling images of uneducated Black girls and women. This stereotype paints Black girls as uncultured, incapable of learning, and without social capital and class, each of which are held to standards of whiteness. The uneducated Black girl eventually becomes the welfare queen, who depends on government assistance rather than a career to afford her lavish expenses and many children with different fathers. Whites benefit from the widespread adoption of controlling imagery through the privilege of their own individualism, but when Black communities also perpetuate these monolithic stereotypes, whiteness is further reaffirmed within nonwhite spaces. The pervasive nature of white racial framing is reinforced, and women who do not fit neatly into controlling image boxes are left cast that way regardless by whites and criticized for not conforming to them by their co-ethnic peers.

Caught between a rock and a hard place, the expectation of conformity to controlling images in white space was expected, but respondents felt particularly hurt when this occurred in co-ethnic spaces. Ravyn, a thirty-year-old Black woman, was one of only three students from her exclusively Black Mississippi high school who attended college. Prior to graduation, the combination of her dialect and good grades resulted in ostracism and bullying from her peers. Rather than priding herself on her academic achievements in school, she blamed them for exposing her as not "Black enough." She recalls, "Because I spoke proper English or because I was a straight-A student, a lot of people did not care for me and thought that because I was quiet or reserved or introverted or whatever, that I was stuck-up. And felt like I was above them. And none of those things are true." Through an intraracial subscription to controlling imagery, the daily message she received from her peers was *you are not really Black*.

Apparent here is that language as a membership marker is not just about languages other than English. In her critical whiteness theory of *ontological expansiveness*, Shannon Sullivan describes how "proper" language, including communication style and tone of voice, is defined by whites.[16] Even in spaces where whites are not physically present, the rules of whiteness still determine belonging and claiming Blackness and Asianness, and are policed by co-ethnic communities to ensure they are upheld. As Shardé Davis succinctly notes, "acting white has nothing to do with wanting to be white and everything to do with what does it mean to be Black."[17]

"You Were Not Black—You Were Something Else"

Systemic racism alienates people of color from one another, and the pervasiveness of white supremacy ensures that anti-Blackness is often ubiquitous in spaces other than white spaces.[18] Pierce spoke of this by-product of systemic racism, noting, "Since Blacks have been victimized to sustain similar attitudes, all too often they, too, adopt pro-racist attitudes and behavior in regard to themselves and to whites."[19] Such attitudes ensure that gatekeeping of white-defined parameters around "true" Blackness, Asianness, and whiteness are still policed in nonwhite spaces. Study respondents spoke to how Blackness was pathologized in Black communities through intentional distancing from other Black families and neighborhoods. In juxtaposition to Andrea's experience with language, Vanesia experienced the opposite; she was expected to reject the AAVE and Southern accent that Andrea was expected to have. As a Nigerian American college student, Vanesia was raised by, and still lives with, her mother in an overwhelmingly white suburb of Atlanta, Georgia. Her mother chose to live in that particular suburb because she believed her children should grow up around whiteness. Vanesia's mother made numerous microaggressive comments and decisions throughout her childhood that implied African Americans were inferior to both recent African migrants living in the United States and white Americans. Vanesia recalls, "Whenever she and her Nigerian friends are talking about their Blackness in America versus African American Blackness in America, they're like, you know, 'Nigerians come here and they're able to succeed like that; why can't these African Americans pull themselves up by the bootstraps and get it together?'"

Here, Vanesia's mother applies the model minority myth to Nigerian diaspora in the United States, implying there is a right and wrong way to be Black in America. Although Blackness is not monolithic, the pathologizing of American descendants of slavery (ADOS) by Vanesia's Nigerian mother communicates to her children that ADOS Black Americans are inferior to more-recent Black immigrants whom she views as "the right kind of Black."

The model minority myth is typically applied to Asian and Asian Americans—usually East Asian—creating an essentialist binary of a right and wrong way to immigrate to the United States. Although some argue that the model minority stereotype is "positive discrimination," it serves to uphold white supremacy by creating impossible standards by which people of color are expected to succeed under the guise of meritocracy.[20] The model minority myth is harmful not only to the Asian Americans it characterizes but also to those with whom they are compared; as the myth goes, if Asians can succeed in the United States with hard work and without challenging the status quo, other minority ethnic groups (coded, of course, Black groups) have no legitimate excuses for their lack of success!

Again, we see evidence of systemic racism's reliance on alienation within a racialized group to maintain white supremacy.[21] This ideology reifies white domination by placing blame on Black Americans for their own experiences of systemic injustice. Rather than acknowledging nearly four centuries of enslavement, legally enforced segregation, redlining, and other unjust disadvantages that have dramatically affected Black success in the United States, Vanesia's mother attributes the conditions of ADOS Black Americans to their own lack of motivation and cultural inferiority. Still, Vanesia shares that her mother has been the victim of microaggressions herself. "It's just the complexity; she's like, are they being this way toward me because they're racist, or is it because I'm African and my accent is thick? Is it imperialist? Colonialist?" Vanesia witnesses her mother's cognitive dissonance when she herself experiences racism from white perpetrators, yet her mother is quick to dismiss these microaggressions as she distances herself further from ADOS Black Americans and takes comfort in this distance.

Black women received microaggressive comments that communicated they were not Black in similar ways of their Black peers. This message was often conveyed to respondents, like Ravyn and Andrea, who were honors students, soft-spoken and introverted, or dressed in modest clothing. These traits specifically defy common controlling imagery of Black women, including the Angry Black Woman, the hypersexual Black woman, and Black women as unintelligent.[22] Like Asian American women, Black women received this message primarily from intraracial peers rather than from family members.

Pierce noted the influence of media perpetuating the stipulations of what it means to be the "right kind" of Black. He studied the way Black characters in film and television are depicted as inferior to white counterparts: a Black detective solves a case with his anger rather than logic in a film; a Black child describes getting eyeglasses as "fun" rather than helping him concentrate and receive better grades in school. Thus, he notes, "the black is seen over and over in such guises as a server and non-thinking physical creature."[23] Media paints Black intelligence as rare and implausible, if not a myth entirely. Sue later outlined the racial microaggression theme *ascription of intelligence* as conveying that someone's intellect is contingent on their race.[24] In recent microaggression research, this is most commonly studied as a component of the model minority myth in which Asian Americans are perceived as good at math and science or high achieving in their finances and careers. For Black women, the opposite assumption is true; Black women are repeatedly microaggressed by the message that their Blackness is equated with inferior intelligence. Even within Black families and communities, this message was widely adopted and implied. Thus, when Black women were successful in school, their peers conveyed that they were the "wrong kind" of Black.

Sailem described the relationship between high academic achievement and Black identity as incompatible. "There's like a level of stupidity. If you were smart and Black in my hometown during elementary and middle school, you were not Black. You were something else." That high-achieving Black girls could not claim their Blackness was implied both overtly and covertly within Black communities, including direct comments and blatant ostracism. These microaggressive messages were twofold: Black girls are never academically inclined, and thus, the ones that are must not really be Black.

Sailem noticed her Black classmates started treating her differently around third and fourth grade, consistent with the first year of gifted and talented programs for elementary schoolers. She was often referred to as "Oreo," a common slight used to describe Black people who are viewed as white adjacent. Similar to the "ABCs" described previously, Oreos are perceived as Black in skin color alone; their behaviors, language, and achievements allegedly personify whiteness. Although Sailem did not internalize this nickname at first, the overarching message eventually affected her when it was perpetrated by intraracial peers:

> Okay, I'm an Oreo; it is what it is. Middle school comes around and I'm really not comfortable with it. I never really had a problem with my Blackness. I never really had a problem with being Black. I had a problem with how people treated me because I was Black. Also, it hurt extra when the people who look like you are saying you're not Black enough because you don't fit this criteria and that criteria. The only difference between me and them at the time was that I had good grades. I read books.

Sailem was comfortable enough with her Blackness to recognize that her peers' treatment of her reflected their own internalization of controlling images. However, typical of most microaggressions, not all respondents were able to pinpoint the intention behind the message. Other Black respondents who were enrolled in gifted and talented programs experienced similar assumptions about the perceived incongruency between Blackness and academic achievement. Chelsea, a Black queer woman in her early forties from Missouri, shared she was once accused of hating Black people by other Black girls because she befriended her white classmates in the gifted and talented program. Briana, also a Black woman, grew up in a well-integrated neighborhood in Augusta, Georgia. She had many Black peers but no Black classmates in the gifted and talented program at her school. Like Chelsea, she primarily spent time with white friends from her classes, whereas her Black peers would not associate with her. When I asked if she tried to befriend other Black students, she recalls, "I don't know. I just feel like I didn't fit in, like I wasn't the right type of Black." This continued throughout high school and college, where she received incessant messages from Black peers that she was not the right kind of Black, not only due to her academic achievements but also her clothing style, hairstyles, social circles, and dialect.

These accounts shared by Sailem, Chelsea, and Briana, and by Andrea prior, again evoke Susan Sullivan's theory of *ontological expansiveness*. White people's historical entitlement to all forms of space ("whether geographical, psychical, linguistic, economic, or otherwise") grants them the power to define the rules of language and communication, defining what is "proper" in regard to tone, dialect, and communication style. [25] While many argue that speaking white, or code switching, serves to privilege people of color from perceptions of inferior intelligence at the time of an interaction, the larger issue is how white-sanctioned definitions of "proper" and "improper" English maintain the supposed superiority of whites in the first place.[26]

Too Light to Be Black

Although language and academic achievement are more nebulous in how people are racialized, skin tone is often the first indication of a person's racial identity before an interaction even occurs between people. As noted, white supremacy, anti-Blackness, and colorism work in tandem to pathologize dark skin and glorify light skin on Black women. Research shows the many privileges light-skinned Black women have over dark-skinned Black women.[27] However, light skin is only privileged inasmuch as experiences of racism are legitimized. White supremacy operates in such ways that make light Blackness prized over dark Blackness as it indicates an association with whiteness. Yet that advantage is precarious, as light Blackness is after all still Blackness.

Light-skinned Black women shared microaggressive messages from intraracial peers that they were not the right kind of Black based specifically on their complexion. Kala is a multiracial queer Black woman with a light skin tone. The interactions she experienced were consistent with anti-Black gendered racism, noting several instances wherein her Blackness was invalidated by other Black peers. These microaggressions were present in romantic relationships, work, and social circles, each communicating to Kala that she was not Black enough to experience anti-Black racism or to participate in Black cultural norms. "There were offhand comments, like microaggressions are, or like, 'Oh my God, I gotta wrap my hair. You know, you don't know nothing about that because you're not really Black' or something like that."

Kala's Blackness was repeatedly questioned as her intraracial peers read her as racially ambiguous. A few years before our interview, she worked as a diversity center advisor at a liberal arts college, where microaggressive comments and questions from Black coworkers and students not only invalidated her Black identity but also challenged her position as an expert in her field. Black students questioned her advising role within Black student associations ("You can't be our advisor if you're not really Black"), and her supervisor, a fellow Black woman, would pick and choose when she acknowledged or dismissed Kala's racial identity. She recalls, "Even though she was a Black woman, I feel like this constant playing up, and dismissal of, and critique of my identity. And my phenotypical appearance was constantly at the fray where I either shouldn't be doing this job because I'm not Black, or I only got the job because I'm Black, or I'm not Black at all and that's why I got the job because I'm an in-between."

For example, Kala shares that this supervisor would send her to sweet-talk a white male facilities worker when her department needed a favor. Kala had previously been sexually harassed by this man and felt her supervisor ignored this experience, instead weaponizing, exotifying, and sexualizing her Blackness when it benefited their department. Other times, her Blackness was downplayed or outright denied by the same supervisor. As her Blackness was repeatedly questioned, Kala gathered that it does not matter how she racially self-identifies; she was perceived by Black students and coworkers as not Black enough to work in a diversity center. Blackness was seen as one thing, and Kala was not it. Yet, while Kala's lighter skin privileged her in many ways, it did not protect her from anti-Blackness.

Conclusion

Unlike Black and Asian women, whites are afforded the privileges of individuality, a tenet only available to the dominant group.[28] As the "unraced" race, whites are allowed to have nuanced experiences, personalities, hobbies, interests, speaking styles, levels of education, and ambitions; these traits reflect who they are as individual people rather than being attributed to their race.[29] Individualism also allows whites to distance themselves from Racists-with-a-capital-R, as *those* are the whites whose individual interests uphold white supremacy in a way that whiteness as a collective allegedly does not. On the other hand, controlling imagery defines who Black and Asian women are expected and allowed to be. Variations from the unintelligent, angry, bad Black mother or the studious, submissive, delicate Asian bride are disregarded as exceptions in favor of the homogenized cookie cutter of Black and Asian women.

White supremacy bestows whites with the power to define the norms of society. Although the microaggressions described in this chapter were perpetrated by my respondents' nonwhite peers and families, the pervasive nature of white racial framing ensures that white dominant ideology continues to advocate the supremacy of whiteness even when whites are absent from the space. Monolithic stereotypes of what defines women of color as truly Black or Asian are shaped by white supremacist ideology to cast racialized others as predictable, uncreative, and inferior to whites. The implication that all Black and Asian women fit into neat categorical boxes ignores the nuance of experiences, personalities, skin tones, hair textures, body shapes, languages, and cultures that exist within Black and Asian communities. Black women and Asian American women who did not conform to predictable and neatly constructed controlling images were excluded and dismissed by their co-ethnic peers and criticized for their personalities, language, and bodies.

Once again, the stories my respondents shared in this chapter demonstrate the impossible position that Black and Asian women are placed in between their own intraracial communities and those outside of them. They are expected to assimilate to whiteness but to also preserve their heritage cultures; they are expected to lighten their skin but also to be dark enough to relate to shared experiences of anti-Blackness. Such expectations place Black and Asian women in unfeasible locations that only further allow whites to define the parameters of what is the "right" and "wrong" way to be Black or Asian in the United States.

CHAPTER 5

Body Talk

Bodies are deeply political. Inasmuch as a body can be racialized, gendered, and sexualized, a body is perhaps the most personal site of political debate. Bodies are highly public and simultaneously private. Bodies influence the experiences of people, and bodies carry people through those experiences. There are no right or wrong ways to have a body, and yet bodies are constantly under critique of rightness and wrongness by both the individual with the body and those outside the individual who perceive the body.

In addition to language and cultural conformity, the belief that "real" Blackness or Asianness must conform to a monolithic standard was communicated to Asian American and Black women by their own families and intraracial communities through *body talk*. When controlling imagery is used to maintain white dominance, women of color are not only expected to behave or speak in the stereotypical ways described in the prior chapter but also to have bodies that confirm the controlling imagery as well.[1] Controlling images are used as instruments of power by exploiting existing gendered, racialized symbols that perpetuate and justify the supremacy of whiteness. These symbols endure through media, reaffirming white womanhood as superior and imprisoning Asian American and Black women into boxes that insist what women of their races *should* look like.

Body talk microaggressions are situated at the intersections of race, gender, sexuality, and thin privilege. They insinuate that not all Asian and Black women's bodies are acceptable for women of their race to have and that all women of color must fit into an idealized shape: one that is rooted in the hegemonic beauty standards that favor white women. Importantly, bodies are inseparable from racialized sexualization. Bodies are often the first location from which one is visually racialized by another, and the subsequent assumptions of the racialized body contribute to sexualization and fetishization of the individual.

For Asian American women, body talk microaggressions from within their intraracial communities implied they should be petite or slender framed. Body talk microaggressions against Black women suggested that they need to be curvy but not fat, and their hair should be loose and straight, not kinky. Consider the contrasting controlling imagery of the Lotus Blossom and the Black Matriarch or Jezebel: the Lotus Blossom is hyperfeminine, submissive, and passive, while the Black Matriarch is angry, loud, domineering, and unfeminine.[2] Although these descriptions do not explicitly describe physical traits, controlling imagery paints a picture of what these women look like. By rendering Asian women as too feminine and Black women as not feminine enough, white women become situated between them as just right, setting the standard for the boundaries of acceptable femininity.[3]

Controlling images are contrasted against European standards of beauty to subjugate Black and Asian American women. Hegemonic standards of beauty act as an operative to white supremacy in which women of color are deemed worthy or unworthy depending on their subscription to hegemonic white femininity. Like masculinity, femininity exists within a hierarchy in which certain types are privileged over others. Mimi Schippers describes *hegemonic femininity* as the heterosexual, middle-class femininity that is typically associated with white womanhood.[4] Hegemonic femininity centralizes whiteness and defines the standards of femininity, including beauty and bodies, of which all women are measured against. Although white women's bodies are also under relentless scrutiny in a patriarchal society, women of color are not afforded the other privileges in political, social, or economic systems that allow white women access to systemized power elsewhere.[5]

Bodies of Color and the Male Gaze

As discussed in the prior chapter, perceptions of the "right" and "wrong" kind of Black or Asian are constructed by white ideologies that discount individuals and instead purport that women of color are, unlike white women, homogenous. In the last chapter, this was evidenced through language, dialect, academic achievement, and skin complexion. Bodies are also measured in this way, measured against controlling imagery of what is considered the "right" kind of body for a Black or Asian woman to have, even in primarily nonwhite spaces. Ravyn is a thirty-year-old Black woman who grew up in a predominantly Black town in Mississippi. As a child, she considered herself a tomboy and dressed casually in T-shirts and tennis shoes. However, as a teenager, her body was constantly criticized by her peers for appearing too masculine. Ravyn recalls,

> I mean like, through high school I was always told I have a flat booty and that I've gotten older. And I was a cheerleader growing up so like, continued to be perpetuated as physique-wise, like I had a lot of muscles and I looked toned and fit, so people say like, I was like a man which, whatever. . . . I did a lot of like overcompensating, so whereas when I was little, I would just wear my tennis shoes and stuff, like as I got older, like at high school, I always tried to make sure that I looked girly so that I didn't get that kind of reputation.

Hegemonic femininity situates women within a gendered and racialized hierarchy wherein white women are considered to possess the ideal physical and personality traits of femininity.[6] Controlling images of Black women as dominating, angry, fat, and simultaneously hypersexualized and desexualized, directly counter these idealized feminine traits. Ravyn internalized the message that her body was masculine to a point of changing her entire clothing style. Rather than the casual tennis shoes and T-shirts she was most comfortable in, Ravyn attempted to feminize her appearance through clothing to validate her womanhood. She further admitted to wearing "booty enhancers" under her clothes to conform to a more accepted image of what Black women's bodies are expected to look like—curvy but only in certain places. When I asked who most often perpetuated the message that she was masculine, she responded, "absolutely mostly Black men" who were not only boyfriends but also friends and peers.

Researchers have found that in comparison to white women, Black women are viewed to possess more masculine traits—a tenet of the controlling imagery of the Angry Black Woman and a reflection of the racial hierarchy within hegemonic femininity.[7] The association of Black women with masculinity upholds white supremacy through both dehumanization and desexualization. bell hooks argues that Black masculinity is shaped by white supremacy, and the subjugation of Black women by Black men (and masculinity) is rooted in the gender norms that were normalized by white society during the Atlantic slave trade.[8] White masculinity is constructed in such a way that prevents men of color from accessing the power associated with it.[9] For formerly enslaved Black men to attempt a reclamation of the traits that depict white-constructed tenets of masculinity as valuable, Black women must conform to the sexist gender roles reflected in white colonial societies. The unwillingness to be further oppressed by co-ethnic men, in addition to white slaveowners, painted Black women as uncooperative, angry, and masculine themselves.[10] Because sexuality is racialized, the anger associated with Black women is inseparable from controlling images of their hypersexuality. If Black women are not seen as "true" women, they are deemed unworthy of the protections that white women receive contingent on their femininity.

Further, many Black women shared how their bodies were overly sexualized by Black peers from young ages. Alicia is a twenty-six-year-old straight Black woman originally raised in New York City. She developed breasts in middle school and discussed the comments her intraracial peers would say about her body, including coining the nickname "Double D." In a specific memory, she recalled a middle school boyfriend who became upset with her when she wore a turtleneck on a field trip. "He didn't have access to my boobs on the trip." The following week, he broke up with her.

Alicia's story may not be different from girls of all races, yet it is important to consider the sociopolitical history within which Black women's bodies are expected to be available to both Black and white men. Annecka Marshall claims the sexualized objectification of Black women is "used by 'white' people and Black men to legitimize [their] sexual and social exploitation."[11] When Black women are depicted as sexually promiscuous and insatiable, their morality and credence are undermined. This weakens Black women's ability to gain social, economic, and structural power that relies on respectability politics.[12] Like sexist gender roles, controlling images of Black women as hypersexual are constructed and normalized by white society, yet the pervasive nature of white racial framing ensures it is internalized and maintained by nonwhite communities as well.[13] She is unable to escape the controlling imagery of the Jezebel even when her clothing does not align with the stereotypical portrait of sexually promiscuous Black women. Instead, her Blackness is what solidifies the projection of this controlling imagery onto her by Black boys and men. Even though the boyfriend never admitted that the modest top was the reason behind the breakup, Alicia felt the message was clear: he was only dating her for access to her body, and when that access was revoked, her value to him was lost.

Sailem recognized this lack of control over perceptions of the body as a lose-lose situation for Black women and girls: "We're responsible for our own objectification. Even the term "fast" usually used for Black girls who are just, their bodies are naturally becoming. You know, you grow breasts and your hips get a little wider and the way you act and the way you always interacted with the men and women within your sphere, is sexualized now; it's like you're actively trying to be sexual, whether or not that's true." For Black girls and women, everyday behaviors like choosing what to wear, politely conversing with a stranger, or maintaining a long-term relationship with a family member or friend are suddenly read as more sexual behaviors than they are intended, simply on the basis of being performed by a Black woman occupying her own body.

Fatphobia as Gendered Racism

In her groundbreaking historical narrative *Fearing the Black Body*, sociologist Sabrina Strings uncovers the racist origins of modern-day fatphobia.[14] Through a complex analysis of art, newspaper clippings, and magazine articles, Strings examines how history, the medical establishment, and white supremacy transformed fatness from once praised to ridiculed on the bases of race and gender. She argues, "The phobia about fatness and the preference for thinness have not, principally or historically, been about health. Instead, they have been one way the body has been used to craft and legitimate race, sex, and class hierarchies."[15]

Although String's work examined the origins of fatphobia within the marginalization of Black bodies in particular, the root of such anti-Blackness resides in white supremacy and the dominance of all bodies of color. White Americans and Europeans were the ones who distanced themselves from racial Others through constructing fatness as greedy, savage, and poor. Given that we understand there is a "right" and "wrong" way to be Black or Asian, insisted on by intraracial communities but ultimately shaped by the white racial frame, women of color are constantly under the scrutiny of a white gaze that demands their bodies conform to a checklist of certain physical traits. For Asian American women, that means a petite, slender physical frame to accompany a petite, slender personality; as perfect war brides, Asian women should be small enough to disappear, both literally and figuratively, behind their white husbands. Clara is not a slender-framed Asian American. At 5′7″, she is also taller than the stereotypical petite Lotus Blossom. Her Viet family showed no reservations opining on her weight, including comments such as "You're so beautiful, but you need to lose weight" and "You'd be so pretty if you just lost your weight." She further describes the fatphobic sentiments she experienced from other Vietnamese people in her job at the nail salon:

> It's really weird because Vietnamese people either think I'm very beautiful because I'm mixed. . . . Or they think I'm very ugly because I'm fat and I could be prettier if I lost weight. And I'm like, okay, that's very extreme. . . . I do get "Oh, you're so pretty because you have a tall nose and it's not flat like ours, blah blah blah." And I have a very defined chin. So they really like that. But then I do get a lot of comments on my weight. And it's very triggering. I hate using that word, but it is very triggering to hear that I'm fat. And I'm just like, why does it even

> matter? Why is that a thing that people hone into when they look at me? And it's only Vietnamese people who do that.

The messages Clara received about her body from other Vietnamese people are twofold: that her body is not acceptable because she is fat, yet she is still more beautiful than other Vietnamese girls because she is half-white and has some typically white facial features. The compliments she received about her nose and chin reinforce the ideology that typically European features are more beautiful than typically Asian features, upholding white women as ideals of femininity and beauty. Still, such indicators of whiteness are not enough to trump her unacceptable weight. This illustrates to Clara that her body is only beautiful inasmuch as it subscribes to white hegemonic femininity.

Clara denies receiving body talk microaggressions from people outside of the Vietnamese community. However, intraracial body talk microaggressions were not uncommon among other Asian American respondents. Yuna, a Korean American woman, felt that her athletic build disappointed her parents, while her sisters had more slender frames. She acknowledged, "I wasn't fat; I just wasn't the ideal shape that [my mother] thought Korean woman should have. . . . I wasn't a hundred pounds." As a high schooler in the 1990s, she was able to adopt the grunge trend of baggy clothes to conceal her natural frame. Still, her parents frequently made slights about her beauty and value as contingent on her weight:

> I'm trying to think when my dad said this. He said, "Yuna would be really pretty if she lost ten pounds." (pause) Like I definitely remember they had a meeting about that. (laughs) And I don't know, I don't think it was like, a meeting centered around that. But it was more, I remember, it was a summer I came back from college, and they were like, "Oh, Yuna is . . . She's doing really well. Yuna is going to be okay. But it would be icing on the cake if she lost ten pounds."

Yuna's parents bought into the media portrayal of petite Asian women and compared their daughters to this controlling image. As a teenager, Yuna internalized the microaggressive message that she did not fit into what Asian women "should" look like to a point of changing her clothing style to downplay her natural shape. When she attended college, her parents included her weight as a measurement of her success in school, communicating that her academic achievement was not enough and that her weight was the defining factor between "doing really well" and "icing on the cake."

Like Asian American women, Black women experienced body talk microaggressions from intraracial peers and family that implied they should adhere to a specific body type that is influenced by white racial framing. Black women reported their family members engaged in fatphobic comments more so than Black peers, indicating that fat bodies were unattractive, unhealthy, and unacceptable. For all the Black women that shared these experiences, comments about their weight were shrouded in concern about their health. Although Sabrina Strings's work demonstrates that anti-fat biases are more suggestive of racial domination than they are about health, there are dramatic and dangerous consequences for those who internalize the equation of fatness with being unhealthy.[16] Zenia described the way her father made the offhand comment "to lay off some food" when she was twelve years old. That comment still impacts her relationship with food today: "It tore me apart. I didn't talk for the rest of the day. I don't think I ever had an eating disorder but maybe disordered eating, where it's not an official thing, but it was very much . . . I even do it to this day. I won't exactly calorie count, but if I have something sweet today, I can't do anything else. Like if I have an iced coffee with caramel or mocha, I can't have much more than that."

Chelsie Dunn, Kristina Hood, and Bianca Owens found that Black women's experiences of gendered racial microaggressions negatively related to their own body appreciation, so it is not surprising that Zenia changed her eating habits after the offhanded slight.[17] Her father claimed the comment was a mere cautionary suggestion reflective of the fact that diabetes runs in their family, though to Zenia, it did not come off as a genuine concern for her health rather than an attempt to police her body to adhere to the white-defined image of femininity. This account was not unusual for Black women; Kala's mother also criticized her weight, veiled under concern for her own health and happiness. Black families policed Black girls' weight through microaggressive comments about diet, clothing, and even the ability to find a romantic partner under the guise of knowing the best interests for Black women. The psychological and emotional aftermath of microaggressions for the target are often contingent on the ways in which perpetrators claim their comment is intended to be good natured. This leaves Black women caught between addressing their perpetrator's true intentions and subsequently subscribing to an Angry Black Woman stereotype only to be dismissed, or ignoring the comment and struggling over the consequences of it for years after the incident.

Especially important here is to recall how gender and racialized hierarchies shape the social acceptability of bodies and how that acceptability changes over time; this allows whites distancing themselves from people of color to justify white supremacy. Perhaps unsurprisingly, the foundations of fatphobia can be traced back to coloniality that reaffirms white patriarchal domination.[18] European colonists argued their own rationality and restraint around food and sex proved their status as the dominant race. In contrast, Black colonized peoples were thought to overindulge, both in food and in sex. The stereotype that Black women are fat, then, is not far removed from the stereotype that they are hypersexual: both reflect a lack of self-control that justifies their subjugation under white colonizer rationality.

The Politics of Black Hair

Black women's hair has been a subject of scholarly research across disciplines for decades.[19] It has been policed, politicized, and debated in media, research, and within Black families and communities. Black hair is inarguably racialized and gendered. The pathologizing of curly, kinky, and natural hair on Black women is often regarded as a tenet of colorism. As such, microaggressions that imply Black women should strive to have "good" hair may overlap with the desire for whiteness. However, I categorized hair under body talk microaggressions due to the nature of other body talk microaggressions that conveyed similar assumptions that Black women can easily alter their bodies.

All twenty of the Black women I interviewed reported receiving microaggressive comments about their hair from other Black people. These comments were double sided: pathologizing natural, curly hair and praising straight, loose hair. The underlying message is that, at least for Black women, naturally kinky hair is unkempt, unruly, and dirty and that straight or loosely curled hair is professional, beautiful, and clean. What should be obvious is that this message does not appear out of thin air; whiteness has shaped the ideals of hegemonic beauty for centuries to emphasize typically white complexions, eye shape, and hair texture.[20] Although the movement to embrace natural Black hair gained popularity in the 1960s and 1970s, followed by a second wave in the early 2000s, the stigma of "good" and "bad" hair, shaped by white racial framing, has not ceased to infiltrate Black spaces.[21] Hair stigmas have resulted in lost jobs, expulsion from school, and denial of employment for Black women and girls with naturally tight, kinky, or curly hair.[22] The pervasive image of "good" hair is rampant in media on popular Black women like Beyoncé and Tyra Banks; it is no surprise pathologizing natural hair has been internalized within Black communities. The Black families and peers of my respondents criticized natural hair in relation to beauty, career opportunities, and romantic success. Sailem, a Black, queer, college student in her early twenties, shares the way her family warned her about the consequences of unaltered hair:

> When I first went natural, my whole family was really against it. Everyone kept saying my hair looked unkempt, or they'll tell me these stories of women who went natural and how their husbands and their boyfriends left them because they

> let themselves go. . . . My granny blow-dried my hair one time, and they told me I look like Don King. Yeah, it was like, really bad. People would constantly ask me, especially early stages when my hair was this short, what I'm going to do about my hair? Even now. Now that I cut my hair, people ask me all the time what I'm going to do with my hair, like I have to be doing *something*.

Similar to Kala's account shared in chapter 3, Sailem is often warned by her family that markers of her Blackness will chase away potential love interests if they are left unchecked. This pressure to maintain straightened hair (for a husband, if not for herself) reflects the way microaggressions are both gendered, raced, and sexualized. Sailem's story further exposes the reigning expectation that Black hair should be altered in some way, even if not specifically through chemical relaxers.

Black respondents rarely shared incidents where their natural hair was blatantly called "bad hair." Instead, the omission of praise of natural hair paired with the excess of compliments when their hair was straightened reveals the ways in which the unspoken may also preserve white racial framing. Kamara, a twenty-nine-year-old graduate student, shared that as a child, her father would only compliment her hair when her mother straightened it. Zenia had a similar experience at age fifteen when she stopped straightening her hair after years of exposing it to heat and dangerous chemicals. "I never would get compliments about my natural hair . . . so I was like, oh my God, do I look ugly? Because people aren't saying anything. And when you're used to getting the constant validation and it's not there anymore, it moves you."

I asked Sailem to describe what "good hair" means in Black families: "Loose hair type. Okay, the closer to European, the better. So if you can't have straight hair, you better have loose curls. You want to look mixed, you know what I mean? Or like you have white heritage." The notion that hair can be "good" or "bad" reflects a larger ideology that bodies in general can be "good" and "bad" as well. Through a desire for "good hair," adjacency to whiteness is once again strived for, while curly Black hair is pathologized as shameful and unruly. Though the sale of chemical hair relaxers has declined in recent years, it is still a $30 million industry that is largely patronized by Black women.[23] Unfortunately, ideologies defining "good" and "bad" hair are not without serious consequences. In 2022, researchers at the National Institutes of Health found that women who used chemical hair straightening products were at a higher risk for uterine cancer compared to those who did not. Of their participants who reportedly used hair straighteners, nearly 60 percent were Black women.[24]

Some Black women's natural hair was already the "good hair," yet they were still exposed to comments from Black friends and family that reflected the foundational anti-Blackness and white supremacy of stigmatized hair. Mya, a twenty-two-year-old queer, multiracial Guyanese woman, claimed she is constantly complimented about her natural lose curls from other Black women as well as Black men. Still, she recognizes these compliments as microaggressions that invalidate other Black women's natural hair. "I don't see it as a compliment at all."

The stigma of natural Black hair as unmanageable further allowed hair microaggressions to be disguised as well-meaning intentions from Black family members and community. Consider how Sailem must have felt as a young girl, her hair compared to Don King's! Black family members utilized hair microaggressions as a tool of respectability politics, associating naturally kinky Black hair with unprofessionalism, insinuating that regardless of one's qualifications, they do not belong in "professional" spaces if their hair does not conform to "good hair" standards. Ravyn is a thirty-year-old program manager at an HBCU (historically Black college). With two master's degrees and a PhD in progress, Ravyn has navigated "professional" spaces for many years, during which she has had both natural and altered hairstyles. At the time of our interview, she has been natural for twelve years, much to the disapproval of her mother:

> My mom hates it. Like, despises it. And every time she sees me, calls my hair nappy. No, it . . . it's a thing. And I tried to reeducate her because I know she grew up in this era, and she, for example, if I have a job interview or whatever, her first thing is, "I hope you're going to straighten your hair" and you know, part of it is, okay, she grew up in that era, and the white racial frame dictates that I straighten my hair in order to get a job and be presentable, quotation marks. And so I need a job and I need to do what is necessary to be able to make myself marketable, but then in my mind I'm like, well, I don't want to work for a place that I can't wear my hair as it grows out of my head! And that would not . . . gel well for her.

A trained sociologist herself, Ravyn acknowledges the permeability of white racial framing on her Black mother's adoption of *respectability politics*. Coined by Harvard professor Evelyn Brooks Higginbotham, the "politics of respectability" refers to the adoption of cleanliness, politeness, and sexual purity by Black people as method to demonstrate that they were capable of engaging in appropriate behavior.[25] Of course, "appropriate behavior" is defined by whites, unstable and changing, and thus responses to any behavior are contingent on the race of the actor and whether they are perceived as belonging in a space.[26] Still, subscribing to respectability politics provides Black people with yet another false promise of protection from white racism. Ravyn's mom insisted that straightened hair would make or break a job interview, and unfortunately, research shows she is not wrong. Most recently, Christy Koval and Ashleigh Rosette found that Black women were perceived to be less professional, less competent, and less likely to be recommended for an interview when their hair was natural compared to both Black women with straightened hair and white women with any hairstyle.[27]

Ravyn's comments demonstrate that such consequences of guarded white supremacy leave Black women, once again, in an impossible location between a rock and a hard place. Ravyn saw this as a problem with systemic racism and not as a problem with her own body but still straightened her hair for interviews to avoid risking the loss of a potential job. While she has worn her hair as natural for years, other Black women described the pain, money, and time they endured to maintain straightened or otherwise altered hair. Two respondents shared how chemical relaxers ruined the health of their hair, resulting in permanent hair loss. The claim that microaggressions surrounding hair were made in the best interests of Black women cannot be rationalized when the very act of straightening their hair causes physical and psychological damage.

Conclusion

Time and time again, we see examples of the predicament Black and Asian American women are in. They are expected to achieve whiteness, to mimic white ideals of beauty but also to be the "right kind" of Black or Asian. Body talk microaggressions are subtle comments or behaviors that communicate a person does not fit within the framework of normalized, celebrated bodies for one's race and gender: that there is a right way and a wrong way, not only to have a body but to present that body to the world. These messages imply that bodies should conform to standards dependent on one's race and gender, that bodies are indicative of women of color's worth, and that typically European features should be strived toward by women of color, even at the expense of their health, dignity, and happiness.

Two particular types of intraracial perpetrators are crucial to recognize in the stories shared about body talk microaggressions above: Black men on Black women, and co-ethnic parents on both Black and Asian American women. While Black women are sexualized by partners and strangers of all races, they are punished for exerting agency over that sexuality. Under chattel slavery, enslaved Black women's bodies were the property of slave owners.[28] Thus, Black women who assert power over their sexuality reflect the reclaiming of their bodies, freedom, and independence, which is perceived as threatening to Black masculinity.[29] Black masculinity must be considered in context of its relation to all masculinities and to Black femininities. Hegemonic masculinity defines "real" men as authoritative, analytical, and forceful, and further depends on femininity to reinforce its superiority; "real" men must have control over women of their racial ethnic groups.[30] Thus, domination over Black women, which includes projecting or removing sexuality from Black women's bodies, is one way that Black men are able to subscribe to this gender ideology as it continues to be reinforced by patriarchal white racial framing.

Further, whether through policing food intake, weight, or hairstyle, co-ethnic parents in particular were often the perpetrators of messages that communicated respondents' bodies were not the right kind of body. Undoubtedly, the role that parents play in respondents' lives, especially when they share a home, is unique from romantic partners, peers, or strangers; from a young age, parental perceptions of "good" and "bad" shape our own and set examples for how to interact with the world around us.

Under a white racial framing, the sexualization of Asian American and Black women's bodies by intraracial peers serve to subordinate women of color within both white and nonwhite spaces. The adoption of white-imposed sexual controlling imagery further leads to adversarial relationships within racial groups that ensure the hegemony of whiteness is not being collectively challenged. Intraracial peers utilized microaggressive comments or behaviors to communicate that Black and Asian American women do not have agency over their bodies or the perception of their bodies, even within co-ethnic spaces. Body talk microaggressions serve to reaffirm the superiority of whiteness by placing contingencies around ways to have a body for Black and Asian American women. The accounts shared reveal how their bodies are placed under scrutiny in intraracial spaces and result in behaviors and practices that put their health, self-confidence, and self-worth at risk.

The prior chapters demonstrate the flexibility and adaptability of white racial framing such that intraracial peers and families perpetuate everyday racism even in nonwhite spaces, yet much of the existing research on microaggressions experienced by people of color are centered on white perpetrators. Pierce first procured the concept of microaggressions with white perpetrators in mind, and the wider scholarship on racisms does tend to default to this interracial dynamic as well. In the next chapters, we shift from intraracial spaces to predominantly white spaces to account for the wide spread of everyday racism beyond intraracial perpetrators.

CHAPTER 6

The Role of Internalized Racism in Interracial Microaggressions

Although people of color in the United States do not have the extent of institutional power that whites have, white supremacist principles permeate nonwhite spaces by enforcing the white racial frame as the dominant ideology.[1] One of the many ways people of color are harmed by white supremacy is through the internalization of white racial framing wherein nonwhites normalize, centralize, and idealize whiteness. This "mental colonialization" or "indoctrination" does not necessarily require the experience of overt racism to internalize a dominant white worldview; it occurs without conscious consent.[2] Thus, although people of color do not hold the institutional power to be racist per se, they can and do internalize white supremacy through this dominant framing and enact it onto others. Put simply, as Ruby Hamad states, "across the world, whiteness has become so attached to the symbols of privilege, wealth, and status that it no longer even needs European-derived white people themselves to perpetuate it."[3]

Chester Pierce uses the acronym STEM to describe how oppressors shape the lives of the oppressed: through control of space, time, energy, and movement.[4] White supremacy affords whites the power to infringe on the STEM of marginalized peoples, leaving them subjugated and terrorized into conforming to the alleged superiority of whiteness. Unconsciously internalizing a white racial frame seems unavoidable for those who are constantly exposed to its parameters and serves a specific function to white supremacist hegemony: the internalization of one's own dehumanization removes responsibility from the oppressor, allowing for continued exploitation.[5] Further, in the United States and other white societies, immigrants and people of color are promised certain societal benefits (including racialized in-grouping) if they assimilate and accept white ideologies, or threatened with ostracism if they refuse.[6] Of course, these promises are often limited, if not entirely empty, to prevent a true reorganization of institutional power; those empty vows ensure that the oppressed support the very parameters that are weapons of their oppression to begin with.[7] Still, the promise of the possibility to escape exploitation is desirable enough to adopt, internalize, and impose on others a white racial framework.

Although internalized oppression varies across groups, psychological research suggests that characteristics of internalized oppression are a common experience among people who have been historically marginalized.[8] Black and Asian scholars such as Frantz Fanon, Karen Pyke, and Malcolm X have discussed this phenomenon extensively. Pierce himself spoke often about the internalization of white supremacy within Black communities as a mechanism for anti-Black perpetuation beyond white borders. He claims, "Powerful active and passive denial mechanisms allow victims to coexist with oppressors, even at the cost of participating in and permitting much of their own catastrophe."[9] Unable to escape ideologies of white domination even among co-ethnics, members of racially marginalized communities are left facing three seemingly inescapable levels of oppression: interpersonal (between individuals), institutional (between themselves and institutions), and internalized (within themselves).[10] Each of these levels works parallel with the others to maintain a constant state of oppression and white dominance. Like all forms of oppression, the manifestation of internalized oppression can be both blatant and subtle, individualized, collective, and institutionalized.[11] Not only does internalized racism influence the way we see ourselves; it influences the way we see our co-ethnic peers as well.

Within-Group Microaggressions

RESPONDENTS AS PERPETRATORS

This unit demonstrated how Black and Asian American communities engage in what E. J. R. Annie Derthick describe as *within-group lateral oppression*: when marginalized people use the dominant (white) societal framework to marginalize others within their own group.[12] Throughout our interviews, respondents often shared accounts of their parents, siblings, peers, and friends inciting gendered racist microaggressions against them that reflected internalized white supremacy and patriarchism: the pressure to assimilate to whiteness, the policing of their bodies, and the classifying of hobbies, clothing, and dialects as not Asian or Black "enough." In these accounts, the microaggressions described embody a nonwhite perpetrator's internal belief that whiteness defines what is normal, what is acceptable, what is exotic, and what gets racialized at all.

However, the awareness of microaggressions that allowed my respondents to recognize them when perpetrated by intraracial family and friends also allowed them to reflect on their own behavior through a new perspective. My respondents frequently shared memories of their own internalized oppression manifesting as microaggressions—incidents where, upon time, distance, and reflection, they recognized their comments were rooted in internalized racism and misogyny. Briana cringes as she shares an incident that occurred when she was an undergraduate attending a predominantly white college in Georgia:

> I was on the bus and there was this Black girl on the bus too. She was a lighter skinned girl, though, not that it really makes a difference, but she was a lighter skinned Black girl. And she was actually an athlete; she was on the track team. And she had on some short shorts and maybe a crop top and she was really loud on the phone. And there was some other white people on the bus whispering, talking about it. So when I was getting off the bus and I passed them, I was like, "Hey, we're not all like that." (pause) And now it's like . . . I can't believe I said that, but I was just like, to be Black, at that moment, so embarrassed.

Briana's own internalized gendered racism caused her to depict another Black woman as loud, unruly, and lascivious: the tenets of the Jezebel controlling imagery. Further, her internalized oppression compelled her to seemingly *apologize* to white people for the (completely normal) behavior and dress of another Black woman. In this moment, Briana incited a gendered racist microaggression against the woman on the bus, one quite similar to the intraracial microaggressions she herself described experiencing at the hands of her Black friends and family.

Several Black women in my respondent pool shared similar accounts; it was clear that unlearning internalized oppression required much more consciousness from my respondents than internalizing it to begin with but that unlearning was being done. Like Briana, Zenia also internalized gendered racist controlling imagery of Black women. She shares, "I had a warped vision of Blackness. I was like, I'm a good Black person. I'm articulate, . . . I come from a two-parent family, . . . obviously I'm better. So my parents both have master's degrees, and I was a smart kid, and being a smart kid already has its own ego associated with it. So being Black and being smart, it's like double team." Here, Zenia's internalized oppression caused her to distance herself from her Black peers, to see herself as "a good Black person" in contrast to a "bad" one, specifically because of her two-parent household, "proper" speech, and academic success—characteristics that are denied to Blackness. Although Zenia was not far out of grade school at the time of our interview, she was able to recognize the role that internalized oppression played in her recent ideology.

Many Asian American women were also able to recognize the influence of internalized oppression on their perspectives of other Asian Americans. Some went so far as to verbally reject their Asian ancestry, such as Lizzie. Lizzie shared that as a child, she often thought to herself, "I don't even like being Korean. I hate all Korean people. They are so backwards; I hate Asian people. Oh my God, I am totally not like them." Annie also distanced herself from her Asian ancestry even in predominantly Asian spaces. Recent-immigrant and U.S.-born Chinese students alike attended a weekend Chinese school where Annie was a student, and she recalls purposefully befriending only those who seemed more Americanized: "We'd be friends because we struggled together and were shitty at Chinese. Like, we cheated in Chinese, it was like that. And we thought we were cool for that, you know? Even the way we dress or the type of music we'd be into and stuff like that. And just being like, 'Oh, this particular Chinese student is so annoying for being so good at Chinese.' It was so stupid, honestly."

Like Briana and Zenia, Annie's internalized oppression caused her to view "white" American traits—like speaking only English—as superior. Interestingly, where Zenia saw academic success as a deciding factor in her status as "a good Black person," Annie internalized the model minority myth to view academic success as un-American—something only her Chinese-born immigrant peers obtained. This speaks to the adaptive nature of white supremacy, which constantly shifts to weaponize identical traits as both acceptable and unacceptable depending on whom they are associated with.

To be completely clear, internalized racism is a consequence of white supremacy, not of a flawed psyche in people of color. Largely studied in context of psychological adjustment, self-image/self-esteem, and in-group attitudes, research on internalized racism has often ignored the structural, macrolevel influence of white racism and hegemony.[13] As Daniel Solórzano and Lindsay Pérez claim, "when racism is reproduced in Communities of Color . . . it is because of the historical legacies of racism and perceived white superiority that have shaped our society. The preference for whiteness we may see shows up in our own families and communities and is bound by centuries-old narratives that white is better, good, civilized, virtuous, beautiful, etc."[14] Internalized oppression must be considered, examined, and critiqued in juxtaposition to the social institutions within which white supremacy is embedded.

Conclusion

Since microaggressions are subtle and ambiguous in nature, targets are more likely to attribute the oppressive nature of their experience as a consequence of personal factors (i.e., "I am being too sensitive") rather than a product of systemic white supremacy. E. J. R. David, Jessica Petalio, and Maria Crouch assert, "This is one way in which microaggressions and internalized oppression are linked: Microaggressions—because of their subtlety and vagueness—are the types of oppression that might be more likely to be internalized."[15]

Internalized racism is born out of anti-Blackness and points to the permeability of white racial framing. Only through an adoption of white supremacist ideologies is internalized racism able to thrive. Pierce explains, "Due to pro-racist attitudes in the United States, both Blacks and whites do things that permit, promote, encourage, sustain, and insist that whites are superior and Blacks inferior."[16]

Although racial microaggression research typically focuses on white perpetrators, and gender microaggression research typically focuses on male perpetrators, the oversaturation of interracial and intergender microaggression research fails to account for the intersectional nature of oppression. My research found that Black and Asian American women are the recipients of gendered racist microaggressions from within their intraracial families and intraracial communities as well. These messages work hand in hand with white supremacy to communicate that whiteness is superior, that women of color must fit into a typecast model, and that women of color's value is contingent on their bodies.

I have outlined four themes in which Asian American and Black women were microaggressed from within their intraracial families and communities; however, the experiences shared within these themes are not mutually exclusive. For example, the pathologization of Black women's natural hair may also fit within the theme of *The Desire for Whiteness*, though I chose to situate it within *Body Talk*. Further, the ways in which families discussed my respondents' bodies may also be situated within the theme *Not Asian/Black Enough*. Each of these instances are encompassed in the overarching theme of gendered racism. Thus, it is essential to consider the ways in which microaggressions perpetrated by intraracial families and communities against women of color are extremely permeable and imply multiple hidden messages when considered collectively.

Within Black communities and Asian American communities exists countless varieties of ethnicities, cultures, and migration histories that cannot be reduced to monolithic experiences. Further, other historically marginalized identities such as citizenship status, sexuality, religion, disability, and class influence the experiences women of color have with microaggressions. Even though I recognize the variation within these communities, I have chosen to examine the experiences of Asian American and Black women as pan-ethnic groups who experience similarities of gendered racialized oppression under a patriarchal white supremacist society. My findings are consistent with Feagin's concept of white racial framing in which communities of color internalize white habitus norms and ideologies, furthering the prioritization of keeping structural power within whiteness.[17] I argue this is also applicable to androcentric norms and ideologies, consistent with my findings of discrepancies between women of color and men. Although there are infinite variations in microaggressions dependent on one's location within a matrix of domination, ADOS, recent migrants, "FOBs," and "ABCs" all experienced gendered racist microaggressions from members of their intraracial communities. Internalized racism, a direct by-product of white supremacy, shapes the ways in which whiteness infiltrates nonwhite spaces, ensuring the hegemony of white supremacist ideology and the dominant white racial frame even in the absence of white actors.

CHAPTER 7

Compliments of the (White) House

Families and childhood homes are often the first institutions to shape who we are and who we will become. For better or worse, families teach us how to interact with others and society around us. As demonstrated in the prior chapters, our families teach us about what is acceptable behavior, what is expected of us, and what is right and wrong.

Five of my respondents identified as women of color but were raised in what they considered to be white households. I define white households as childhood homes in which one or both parents of the respondent who reside in the home are racialized as white. White households may also include white siblings, step-siblings, and grandparents who live within the home but do not include current white spouses or in-laws as the focus is on relationships with family members that are developed in childhood. I focus on three of the five women, who each grew up in different types of white households.

The Myth of an Unmarked Whiteness

A common exercise in Introduction to Sociology and Race and Racisms classes is to ask students a self-reflective question: At what age did you first become aware that you were a member of your race? In my own classroom, I have asked my students to consider this question many times. The answers are usually predictable, even across quite different classrooms; students of color become aware of their race, or at least of their nonwhiteness, much earlier in their lives than white students. While students of color recall early childhood memories of racist name-calling from peers or translating English for their parents in their native tongue, white students more often did not consider their whiteness until high school or even college years. I have even had students share they did not have to think about their whiteness until that very exercise.

Such consistency speaks to the myth of an unmarked whiteness; as education systems teach white history, medicine reflects white research, and the dominant perspective in the United States centers a white racialized framework and habitus, it is no surprise that white students rarely had to consider what it means to be white. Why would they? Whiteness is seen as the default race; normal is equated with whiteness, and those who do not fit within boundaries of whiteness are deemed the racial Other. Whiteness is the unraced race. But herein lies the myth: Whiteness is structured in dominance.[1] Whiteness is not unmarked to people who must navigate white space and interactions with white people.

Scholars of race and racisms debate the unmarked nature of whiteness; if whiteness is the default ideology, the norm, the standard by which we are all expected to subscribe to, yet we don't name it as whiteness, it is arguably invisible. To have and exercise power includes both power to name (thus, to other) and to remain unnamed. Still, many scholars contest this claim, arguing that for nonwhite people, whiteness is incredibly apparent. Sociologist Elijah Anderson defines *white space* as "a perceptual category" that is considered off-limits, uncomfortable, or unapproachable for Black people.[2] Whiteness as a location, white space, is quickly noticeable for those who are marginalized within it, though it may be unremarkable for whites, who are not in physical or social danger inside its boundaries.

In their own analyses of white spaces, David Brunsma and colleagues note, "White spaces are not always characterized by the absence of people of color, rather they are spaces where culture is deployed in ways that secure white racial interests and subordinate nonwhites."[3] White spaces are not necessarily physical locations that are formally or even informally segregated; instead, they are places where the normalization, domination, and standardization of whiteness persists. White space may embody neighborhoods, workspaces, schools, doctor's offices, retail spaces, or other public areas, and is reinforced by both the institutions it occupies and interactions within it.[4] People of color within white space are often viewed as "out of place" for even daring to occupy it.[5] Although it is possible to try to limit the amount of time we spend in white space, we all must, at some point, go to a doctor, shop for something outside of our neighborhoods, navigate education and work systems, or find ourselves in other public or private institutions that are predominantly white. Because of the pervasive nature of white space, it is difficult, if not impossible, for people of color to avoid traversing it entirely.[6]

In contrast, spaces that are deemed safer (or at least more comfortable to occupy) for people of color have been called counterspaces, Black spaces, or homeplaces.[7] As long as there has been white space, there has been the construction of counterspaces that allow people of color, and specifically women of color, the comforts of reaffirmations, resistance, and recovery from the exhaustion of constantly negotiating white, male, and oppressive spaces.[8] For many, these counterspaces are among co-ethnic communities, neighborhoods, and family. Of course, my respondents demonstrated in the prior unit that nonwhite communities are not immune to white racial framing and white supremacist ideologies, yet these co-ethnic home spaces are still more endurable than exclusively white space. But what if your own home was also white space?

Color-Blind Parenting

SUNNIE, A KOREAN AMERICAN ADOPTEE

Sunnie is a Korean American adoptee in her early thirties who grew up in the Southwestern United States. She has two older white siblings and one younger white sibling, none of whom are adopted. Raised by two white parents, Sunnie was the only nonwhite person (and the only adoptee) in her childhood home. Although she shared that her family members made many attempts to be racially aware and inclusive, they still engaged in color-blind microaggressions that reflect the adoption of white racial framing and white ideological dominance, which led to racially othering Sunnie within their white household.

Eduardo Bonilla-Silva defines *color-blind racism* as an ideology that explains the consequences of modern racism as a result of nonracial dynamics.[9] Adopting color-blind racism requires the embracement of meritocracy, essentialism, cultural inferiority, and the minimization of racism to explain social phenomena that are the by-products of centuries of racist laws, policies, and ideologies that uphold white supremacy. Color blindness specifically allows whites to ignore the legacy of racism and settler colonialism on the lived experiences of people of color in the United States. Insisting that race is insignificant in terms of academic, career, financial, or social success discounts the way white supremacy is institutionalized and legally and covertly reinforced. Within a white racial framework, white and nonwhites alike have adopted color-blind racist ideologies to distance themselves from overt racism and take comfort in the belief that how a person is racialized is no longer relevant in gaining social, political, and economic success.

However, although race is a social and political construct, the consequences of race are very real. The way we are racialized shapes the lives of all of us, including white people. In a country that was founded on white supremacy through

Indigenous genocide and an entire economy built on the enslavement of Black people by whites, race is arguably one identity factor that has consistently and relentlessly mattered throughout U.S. history.

When color-blind racism is enacted through microaggressions, the message is that one's race is insignificant to their life events and that their experiences, obstacles, and privileges are a result of their own efforts or failures of success rather than nonwhites' realities being influenced by unjust systemic barriers. The unjust enrichment of whites, and subsequent unjust impoverishment of Black and brown people, are thus chalked up to meritocracy and smart decisions rather than an inescapable and ongoing history of systemic racism.

Sunnie's parents occasionally acknowledged the significance of her identity as Korean American in an all-white household. She recalls how her parents tried to honor her Korean ancestry by occasionally attempting to prepare traditional Korean foods. However, these efforts were sporadic rather than transformative of Sunnie's racial socialization, indicative of "well-intended but problematic" cultural tourism that reduced Korean identities to nonthreatening foods and holidays.[10] In their work on Korean adoptees, Jiannbin Shiao, Mia Tuan, and Elizabeth Rienzi found this behavior common for white parents of adopted Korean children; occasional token gestures were scattered among the predominantly white, and color-blind, upbringing.[11]

Color-blind microaggressions were both spoken and unspoken by Sunnie's family. She recalls her parents' limitations and discomfort of addressing racial difference that pointed to their comforts with color blindness. For example, when her younger brother was born, her parents bought each of their three older children a baby doll of their own. Sunnie's older sister and brother received white baby dolls with light blond hair, a common doll available at any toy store in the early 1990s. But Sunnie's doll was Black. She recalls the pain she felt in realizing her own doll was different from her siblings':

> I was kind of offended that my baby doll did not look like my sister's or my brother's baby. . . . Like, a brown baby, not super dark, but you know, tan. So looking back, I'm like, probably that's something that, if I had been more aware I would have appreciated, but at that point, that was just a marker of me being different. So I didn't appreciate that. And they took that doll back immediately and got me the one that, you know, I felt I looked like, I wanted to look like. But I think that's when I realized that oh, I guess, like anything out in the world, things out in the world that represent who my family is, what my family looks like, don't represent what I look like.

Sunnie's parents matched her siblings' skin tone and hair color with blond, white dolls, but in an attempt to account for her racial difference, paired with a lack of Asian baby dolls on the market at the time, they conflated her Asianness with general nonwhiteness and assumed the Black doll represented her racial identity more so than the white dolls. The conflation of nonwhiteness with Blackness illustrates the normalization of a racial binary where whiteness is the only race deemed worthy of individualism—everyone else is just *other*. The U.S. census did not even acknowledge races other than white and Black until seventy years past its inception with the inclusion of Indigenous Americans, and the undistinguished category "Asian" was not included until another decade after that.[12] Yet, toy manufacturers were even further behind. For example, it was not until 1995 that Pleasant Company's *American Girl* line debuted their first Asian doll on the market, almost a decade after their first productions[13]—and years after the birth of Sunnie's little brother. The baby dolls on the market at the time were primarily white or Black. To Sunnie's parents, being Asian was surely not white, so if given a choice of a white or Black doll, Sunnie's parents chose Black.

This choice was not made in a vacuum—in the United States, Asians have a long history of being conflated with Black groups both socially and legally. Sociologists Rosalind Chou and Joe Feagin describe how, in the nineteenth and early twentieth centuries, Asian immigrants in the United States experienced both blatant individual and institutional racism, cast as "black" or "near black," with similar associated dangers and crimes as Black Americans.[14] Histories of Black and Asian immigration to the United States and beyond—both forced and voluntary—further complicate racial boundaries that attempt to classify people into discrete racial categories. Although we see more inclusion of racial diversity today, the conflation of nonwhite groups as a monolithic Other persists. This results in a consensus among whites that there is white, and there is everything else.

As an adult, Sunnie admits with some discomfort that the white doll was preferable to her than the Black doll despite the fact that neither looked like her. Perhaps in a world of isolated incidents, this could be chalked up to what she posits is solely a "marker of being different." But we do not live in such a world, and as a young child, Sunnie had already internalized the white racial framing that permeated her household, viewing the Black doll as undesirable compared to her siblings' white counterparts. This preference evokes memories of the Clark doll study, made notorious in their influence in supreme court cases that argued against racial segregation.[15] In a series of "doll tests," psychologists Kenneth and Mamie Clark aimed to study the psychological impacts of segregation on Black children. During these tests, Black children were asked to identify which of two dolls, identical in every way except skin color, they preferred. Most children not only preferred the white dolls but also attributed positive characteristics to the white dolls (the good doll, the nice doll) and negative characteristics to the Black ones (the bad doll) despite also recognizing their own similarities to the Black dolls. Perhaps the most damning finding from the Clark doll studies is the fact that Black children were shown to be aware of their "inferior status" in American society by age five.[16]

Nearly half a century after the Clark doll studies, for a five-year-old Korean adoptee in a growing all-white family, a Black baby doll still represented more than mere plastic and cloth. Receiving the Black doll communicated to Sunnie that she was not the same as the other members of her family, and the lack of conversation surrounding the doll further conveyed that speaking about these differences was taboo. Sunnie's story is a clear example of the *exceptional belonging* experienced by Korean adoptees. Coined by sociologist SunAh Laybourn, exceptional belonging describes Korean adoptees as "extraordinarily equipped for inclusion through culturally constructed narratives of deservedness while also being routinely identified for exclusion."[17] Sunnie's parents teetered between homogenizing all nonwhiteness in attempts to be race conscious, and hiding behind the comforts of color blindness when it did not work out: rather than explain what it means to be white, Black, or Asian in response to Sunnie's upset, they quickly exchanged the Black doll for the same blond, white doll and never spoke of it again. By avoiding a conversation about race, her parents reinforced the ideology that whiteness is unraced. Describing the consequences of color blindness by white parents, Shannon Sullivan writes that it allows parents "to avoid clumsy and difficult conversations about race and white domination in which they fear they will say something inadequate, wrong, or harmful about race or racism."[18] Although avoiding the discussion saves parents from their own discomfort, "such lessons implicitly teach [nonwhite children] that race is bad, which can encourage a self-deprecating internalization of white superiority given that nonwhite people are seen as quintessentially raced."[19]

The reality is that color blindness, regardless of the alleged good intentions in implementation, does not benefit transracially adopted children in white families. Transracial adoptions and racially blended families, regardless of the presence of adoption or not, are highly controversial. Shiao, Tuan, and Rienzi found that the majority of white parents who adopt Korean children engage in color-blind parenting approaches that serve to racially socialize Korean kids as "honorarily white" rather than as truly, impossibly, color-blind.[20] *Honorary whiteness*, described by Bonilla-Silva, categorizes marginalized racial groups who are not white but experience economic and social privileges and tend to socialize primarily with whites rather than those in what he refers to as the collective Black.[21] However, so-called honorary whites will never benefit from every privilege of whiteness, regardless of how strongly parents attempt to instill white norms and downplay the significance of race in their lives.

Sunnie now proudly wears "Asian American Girl Club" hats, has "#VeryAsian" hashtag in her social media bios, and prepares vegan iterations of her favorite Korean foods regularly. She claims her own college and graduate education in philosophy and gender studies allowed for "an awakening" in which she learned to think critically about her experiences with racialized sexism and has dismissed the ideology that discussing such things, especially with family, are inappropriate or taboo. Whether that sentiment is shared, however, is another story.

Sunnie receives color-blind microaggressions from other white members of her family beyond her parents. Her older white sister internalized the color-blind ideology present in their upbringing and now inflicts gendered racist microaggressions through a color-blind lens. In one conversation with her older sister, she recalls explaining a specific gendered racist microaggression that she is often subjected to at the hands of white men. Her example led to a debate regarding multiple marginalized identities and how women of color experience sexism at the intersection of racism within a matrix of domination. In one exchange, her sister pushed back when Sunnie explained that sexism is also inherently racialized: "I asked her, 'Have people ever made a comment towards you, strangers on the street, that was in another Asian language because they assume that that's what you speak? Or said something about how they want you to "love them long time," and all of that?' And she was like, 'Yes!' as if that meant when it was spoken to me, it wasn't racist."

The catcall Sunnie is describing demonstrates the intersecting nature of gender and race with controlling images of Asian American women as the China Doll: sexually available but only to white men. The phrase is unfortunately familiar to perhaps nearly all Asian American women, though almost forty years later, the source material may not be. Stanley Kubrick's 1987 war film, *Full Metal Jacket*, follows a group of U.S. Marines into Da Nang, Vietnam during the Tet Offensive. In a scene that barely spans two minutes, actress Papillon Soo Soo (who is ethnically Chinese) portrays a Vietnamese sex worker soliciting American GIs—a nod to the frequent engagements of American military men with South Asian sex tourism during the Vietnam War. As she sways around their table and negotiates her rate, she repeats, "Me so horny!" and "Me love you long time!" while offering the white men "everything you want" for ten dollars. The men laugh and mock her. The film received favorable reviews, several nominations for awards, and won Best Adapted Screenplay in 1988.[22] But at nearly two hours long, this brief encounter is the most indelible. Two years after the film's release, hip-hop group 2 Live Crew released a song, "Me So Horny," which also included samples of Soo Soo's dialogue from the film and reached Billboard Hot 100 for thirty weeks.[23] Since then, these two phrases have appeared across various forms of pop culture media including Sir Mix-a-Lot's Billboard hit "Baby Got Back," *South Park* (season 2, episode 13,

"Cow Days"), *The 40-Year-Old Virgin* (2005; dir. Judd Apatow), and Fergie's "London Bridge." Although merely a two-minute scene, the cultural impact of these phrases has followed Asian American women well into the next thirty years.

Yet Sunnie's sister claims she, as a white woman, faces the same catcalls that are racialized and sexualized specifically about Asian women. This microaggression reifies one of Bonilla-Silva's central tenets of color-blind racism: the minimization of racism.[24] Her claim invalidates Sunnie's experiences with these catcalls as gendered and sexualized racism and suggests that sexism in general is truly colorblind. Not only does this reflect her sister's vehement adoption of color blindness and reject the significance of Sunnie's intersecting gender *and* race; its believability is also questionable—are white women typically catcalled with the broken English of "Me love you long time" and "Ni hao" as often as Asian women? And if they are, are the consequences for white women the same?

The minimization of racism within the larger context of sexism embodies what Chicana feminist Elizabeth Martínez referred to as *Oppression Olympics*.[25] Oppression Olympics describe a propensity for marginalization to be seen as competitive: one's marginalization is deemed more or less oppressive than another's and must be justified through competition. Of course, women of all races are subjected to some form sexism in a patriarchal society, but the ways in which that sexism meets classism, racism, ableism, cisheterosexism, nationalism, and other forms of discrimination are not universal for all women. It is imperative to understand that privilege and oppression are not mutually exclusive; our marginalized identities do not neutralize our privileged ones. In this incident, Sunnie is trying to explain to her white sister that her experience with sexism is contingent on her race; Sunnie's sister insists that her own experience with sexism is identical to Sunnie's, and therefore race cannot be a true factor. Ultimately, Oppression Olympics serve to maintain white supremacy and domination; if marginalized groups are arguing with one another about who has it worse and who is most justified in their upset, they are not building alliances, coalitions, and solidarity to dismantle white supremacist patriarchy. White women's propensity to engage in Oppression Olympics is discussed further in the next chapter.

Orientalism

CLARA, A BIRACIAL VIETNAMESE AND WHITE AMERICAN

Sunnie was the sole nonwhite member of a household with five other white family members within it, so it is easy to see how whiteness shrouded her experiences with microaggressions, color blindness, and white racial framing. But blended racial households are not unusual, and they don't all look like Sunnie's. Clara is a twenty-eight-year-old biracial woman who was raised by her white father and Vietnamese mother in a Southern suburban town. Although her father was the sole white family member in their house, his comments, rules, and demeanor as "head of the household" still ensured white racial framing was the dominant ideology within their home.

When Clara was a child, she remembers a peaceful household in which her father encouraged her to learn Vietnamese from her mother and to take part in Vietnamese traditions. However, her mother's sister later immigrated from Vietnam to the United States and lived with the family for several years. Clara recalls how her father's demeanor toward Vietnamese women changed after her aunt moved in.

> I guess my dad thought my mom changed or something. I guess it was just being with her sister who was in Vietnam for you know, forty-something years and adjusting to always eating fried stinky fish, which I love. But, you know, he was just like, we have this new house and now it just smells like fish all the time. And basically all of our savings went into bringing her here. And I think that's kind of where the resentment came from. And it changed my mom and made her more Asian, more Vietnamese.

Clara shared that she enjoys cooking and eating traditionally Vietnamese foods but that her father engaged in microaggressions that pathologized the cultural value of those foods. Her mother migrated to the United States from Vietnam as an adult and has always spoken Vietnamese, cooked Viet foods, and celebrated her heritage. Although her father was welcoming of Clara learning to speak Vietnamese, to celebrate Viet holidays, and to engage in Vietnamese culture, these must be done on his terms; if the household becomes too Vietnamese, *too Asian*, these cultural norms become a source of resentment.

Clara's statement makes clear that she has internalized some of the messages she received from her father: that her Vietnamese mother somehow became "more Asian" spending time with her sister. The implication here is that "more Asian" is less white, less American, and less pleasant to be around as her father's resentment grows. Keep in mind, both women spent the majority of their lives in Vietnam before migrating to the United States as adults; they *are* Vietnamese. Yet, the message Clara received from the microaggressive comments of her father implied that becoming "more Asian" was something to resent. This resentment seemed to exacerbate around the 2016 presidential election.

> I've had fights with my dad. It was over Donald Trump too, every fight we have is over politics. And I just remember one day I was like, "You're racist," and he's just

> like, "Oh, you think I'm racist? I'm not gonna talk to you anymore." I don't even remember what it was. It was probably just some dumb shit. He has called me a chink before but not . . . He's just like, "Haha, you're just a chink!" and then I'm like, "Ha!" And we will both laugh about it. It depends on the context. He's never said it when we're fighting, but sometimes he'll be like, "the Blacks," and I'm like, that really irks me. "Why do you have to say it in that way? Why can't you be like, Black people? Or African Americans?" but it's always just like, "the Blacks." It's just like, the way he says it really fucking pisses me off. And I don't know, I don't want to be like, he's racist, but those are things that racist people say.

Clara views her father's comments as "things racist people say" rather than name him explicitly as racist. Here, she tries to rescue her father from the label of Racist-with-a-capital-R, though his comments paint a different picture that she admits anger her. Still, it's easier for Clara to dismiss his racism when it takes the form of microaggressions.

Further, the discrepancy between what Clara views as excusable in her father's language is important. Clara considers herself politically progressive and can recognize—and even challenge—when her father engages in anti-Black microaggressions. However, she dismisses a derogatory anti-Asian slur as playful. Throughout their interviews, it became clear that Clara and Sunnie both recognized anti-Black microaggressions as racist but had more difficulty framing anti-Asian rhetoric in the same way. Sunnie admitted this was due to the color-blind framing of her upbringing and actively attempts to resist this tendency in adulthood. Clara, however, internalized the anti-Asian microaggressions her father perpetrated and often excused and dismissed his gendered racism against Asian women more so than she did when he engaged in anti-Black microaggressions.

One toxic device of white supremacy is the way in which oppressed groups are pitted against one another to ensure the stability of white dominance. This is evident in the Oppression Olympics praxis that Sunnie's sister engaged in, and further in the ways Black and Asian American race relations exist today. This practice ensures that regardless of how racialized privileges and oppressions ebb and flow, whiteness remains socially dominant and unchallenged above all other races. All nonwhite peoples are marginalized within a white supremacist structure. How that marginalization looks, however, varies. Asians and Asian Americans have been impacted by anti-Blackness in the United States. Asians and Asian Americans have *also* benefited from and engaged in anti-Blackness in the United States; both can be true. This does not negate their own oppression within the confounds of white supremacy but instead points to the calculated and complex way that macro social forces influence relationships between micro and meso affiliations like individuals and communities. When groups of color are busy pointing fingers against one another, no one looks at who is pulling the strings.

Clara views her father's anti-Blackness as problematic but less so his use of racial slurs and microaggressions against Asians. The only exception to Clara's dismissal of her father's anti-Asian sentiments during our interview surrounded his comments about predominantly Asian spaces at the beginning of the COVID-19 spread in March 2020.

> I'm like, "Oh, let's go to Lin's Bistro," which is a local Chinese restaurant. And this was before, you know, we were on lockdown. And he's just like, "That's the last place I'd want to eat right now." And I'm like, why? We've been going to them for years and just because it's a Chinese restaurant doesn't mean anything. And I feel like I've gotten a lot of shit from him because my mom and I went to H Mart which is the Korean Market. And he was just like, "Jesus Christ. Why would you go there?" I'm like, what's any different than Kroger? At least they have the shields protecting the customer and the cashier!

The COVID-19 pandemic served as an opportunity to understand how the concept of honorary whiteness is unstable. The alleged Chinese origin of the virus, paired with the incessant anti-Asian rhetoric of Donald Trump in media, engaged monolithic stereotyping and cast all Asian Americans (including, but not limited to, Chinese Americans) as unclean, dangerous, and forever foreign. Stereotyped as the "good minority" for the past several decades, the pandemic reminded us that whiteness calls the shots and that a racial hierarchy is malleable so long as whiteness remains on top. Many Asian Americans experienced increases of both microaggressive behavior and blatant, violent racism from non-Asians.[26] Violence and racism against Asian Americans has been part of U.S. history for centuries, yet model minority controlling imagery has minimized or fully erased anti-Asian violence from public discourse since the 1960s.[27] However, the COVID-19 pandemic caused a rise in anti-Asian racism in both covert and overt attacks; in the first quarter of 2021, the largest U.S. cities experienced a 164 percent increase from the year prior in physical violence inflicted on Asian Americans.[28] Although harassment, shunning, and violent acts were inflicted on Asian Americans collectively, Asian American women in particular saw over twice as many violent incidents during this time as Asian American men.[29]

The importance of this distinction and the use of an intersectional lens is no better demonstrated than in the March 16, 2021 murders of six Asian and Asian American women in Atlanta, Georgia. Four Korean women and two Chinese women were murdered by a twenty-one-year-old white man, Robert Aaron Long, who claimed he saw them as temptations of his sexual addiction.[30] Although Long claimed the attacks were not racially motivated, the businesses he targeted and witness statements recounting his anti-Asian rhetoric during the attacks make this claim unlikely. This event cannot be fully understood outside of context of the frequent sexualization of Asian women, paired with these particular women's working-class occupations and the rise of anti-Asian sentiments in the United States at the time of the murders; Asian and Asian American women in sexualized, working-class occupations are viewed as dirty, un-American, and ultimately, disposable.

Once viewed as the model minority within honorary whiteness, Asian Americans, many of whom are second, third, and fourth generation in the United States, are still regarded as un-American. Within a white racial frame, they may both benefit from and suffer under anti-Blackness but never gain the full privileges of whiteness. The COVID-19 pandemic exacerbated this forever-foreign ideology, and sentiments such as those of Clara's father justify both blatant racism and anti-Asian microaggressions. The message Asian Americans received from physical assaults, subtle comments, and jarring stares communicated that regardless of their citizenship status or inability to speak Asian languages, they did not belong and they were not safe. Her father's casual use of racial slurs, disgust and fear of Asian grocery stores and restaurants, and resentment toward his wife becoming "more Asian" all demonstrate the malleability and fleeting nature of honorary whiteness. His microaggressive comments further reinforce the white dominating ideologies present in his household. Asians can be Asian in the United States but only on white terms.

Gas "White"-ing

SERENA, A BIRACIAL BLACK WOMAN

The sense of belonging and not belonging was especially difficult for respondents who felt alienated within their own homes. Serena is a twenty-three-year-old biracial Black woman whose parents are divorced. She spent most of her childhood in California living with her white mother, her white stepfather, and her white half brother.

Pierce notes a trademark tenet of microaggressions is that the incident at hand may seem inconsequential, but the "relentless omnipresence" and daily accumulation of each act are what make microaggressions toxic to body, mind, and general well-being.[31] The previous chapters identified co-ethnic communities and families as culprits of using gendered racist microaggressions, making many women of color feel unsafe from perpetual everyday gendered racism. For children of color in white households, this feeling is twofold; similar to co-ethnic family and peers, the adoption of a white racial frame drives white families to engage in gendered racist microaggressions against girls of color. However, in white households, race is often not considered a salient identity. This allows whites to maintain the illusion of color blindness and preserve whiteness as the default unracialized race.[32] Unfortunately, familial color blindness in a white habitus can hinder girls of color's understanding of how their early experiences are racialized and gendered. Serena describes an incident from childhood that has vividly stuck with her over a decade later:

> This one thing may seem like not a big deal, but it definitely was. I was probably twelve, and I was at my mom's house, and she was having a birthday party for my little brother. And so basically, a bunch of white families were coming over and I had one of my friends with me who was white. And my mom asked me to open the door for people. And I am greeting people at the door and like, literally I didn't even open the door for one family, before I get to this family, I opened the door and they just stare at me, literally they don't even say hello. They don't say "Is this the party, is this the right house?" They're just like, a mom, dad, and kids they're all just like . . . they couldn't believe! And I didn't know what to do. And then my mom comes and opens the door so she shows herself. And they go, "Oh, now we know we're at the right house now." . . . Why would a brown girl be at the party anyway? And then for the rest of that party I just became hyperaware of it. I was like, "Wow, this is how they see me." Despite the fact my pictures are all over this house, people were asking my friend, my white friend, "Oh, so you're Jonah's sister!" And although that wasn't the first instance of overt racism like, "I hate Black people," it was still like, "Oh my God, I am *other*."

Although this incident was not dealt by Serena's immediate family, she associates the feelings of this memory with a sense of not belonging—of being *other*—in her white household. The visiting white family's expressions of surprise and confusion communicated to Serena that a mixed Black girl does not belong in a white family's home; her body was perceived as out of place in this white space.

Serena understood that when isolated, this incident may be perceived as a one-off slight in her life; she even qualifies the story by ensuring the interviewer understood this as "definitely a big deal." Such is the skillful craft of everyday racism: racist incidents are so routine that targets feel rationalization is necessary to explain the emotional ramifications. From a critical race theoretical perspective, microaggressions serve to maintain a larger system of racism: white patriarchal supremacy. Serena's anecdote is situated within an accumulation of microaggressive events in her life that predicate on her belonging to a white household, including being mistaken for her brother's nanny or being perceived as adopted by two white parents. The cumulative effect of such incidents points to a broader message that Black girls do not belong in white space—unless they are servants or guests to whites—leaving Serena emotionally taxed and feeling like "the *other*."

Everyday racism is so fully integrated into routine, daily practice that it often appears unremarkable.[33] This further ensures microaggressive comments and behaviors are easy to dismiss as unracialized. Broadly, the act of gaslighting refers to a manipulative psychological tactic that distorts a person's perception by denying their reality, making them feel "crazy." Although often understood as a behavior between two people, at its core, gaslighting relies on macrolevel social inequities.[34] In particular, Angelique Davis and Rose Ernst define *racial gaslighting* as "the political, social, economic, and cultural process that perpetuates and normalizes a white supremacist reality through pathologizing those who resist."[35] Racial gaslighting relies on narratives that obscure the existence of white supremacy as a dominant power structure in the United States. Paige Sweet extends the study of gaslighting further into sociological territory, arguing that gaslighting is also a gendered phenomenon when we consider the imbalance between women and men in political, economic, and cultural capital.[36] Extending intersectional theory and everyday racism into the concept of racial gaslighting and racial spectacles, gendered racialized gaslighting is a process that normalizes white supremacist patriarchy and obfuscates the realities of women of color in particular. Unlike blatant sexist racism, gendered racial microaggressions leave women of color gaslit by the enactors, their experiences with gendered racism minimized or denied entirely.

Of course, a shared, invested stake in whiteness ensures that it is not only the perpetrators that engage in gaslighting; other whites employ gaslighting on behalf of their ilk to maintain their vested interest in white domination. Bonilla-Silva proposes that whites live within a *white habitus* that fosters racial solidarity among themselves.[37] This habitus is evident through white segregation and whites' adoption of color blindness that ensures they do not view such isolation as racialized at all. Instead, the white habitus allows whites to see themselves in a positive light, their condition a product of happenstance rather than a legacy of white supremacy. For example, Serena attempted to discuss the birthday party incident with her mother after the party was over. She recalls, "When I told her about it, she was like, 'No, they're not racist because they didn't mean it.' Well, I don't know how they meant it, but because she thought they didn't mean it like that, because they're nice people, then it wasn't racist? I was like, it literally, it is. You can *feel* it."

Here, Serena's mother engages in a microaggression herself by dismissing Serena's experience as unrelated to race. This minimization of racism reifies her mother's adoption to color blindness. Her response communicates to Serena that incidents she perceives as racialized are not truly racialized and that Serena's account of the incident is thus inaccurate. Serena's account is more than just her recollection of a confused look on a white family's face; the lasting effect so familiar of microaggressions ensures that she "*feels* it." Furthermore, the relationship her mother ties between "nice people" and racism is one all too familiar.

Serena's mother assumed that because *she* did not perceive Serena's experience as a racist event, it must not be racialized at all. The white household within which she raised her family reflects the white habitus that conditions her view of the world. Yet, as Sullivan notes, color-blind parenting is especially harmful on kids of color "because childhood is a crucial time for the formation of a person's racial habits."[38] If white parents are unable to conceptualize race as a salient identity for their children, girls of color are left without the tools and language to combat the message that they do not belong within their own families. Not only does this reimpose feelings of not belonging on a micro level; the macro implication points back to the domination of whiteness. The fact that Serena's white family did not discuss racial matters at all prevented them from acknowledging the validity in her lived experience and the harm, whether covert or overt, that white people have caused on Black women. Serena's mother claimed the white family's actions were not racist because the intention to cause harm was not present. However, the nescience of their shock was precisely what defines their behavior as everyday racism. In her color-blind microaggressive response, Serena's mother failed to acknowledge the hidden ways racism manifests, regardless of intent.

Conclusion

Evidenced by these accounts, wherein their own time at home is not protected from microaggressive comments that reinforce the superiority of whiteness and their subordination to it, we must wonder if we can ever be truly safe from everyday racism. Many respondents' earliest encounters with microaggressions were within their own homes, where the color blindness, Orientalism, anti-Blackness, and racial gaslighting were taught as par for the course in white space. White racial framing is so normalized that whiteness is deemed race neutral or unraced at all. This approach embodied parenting strategies and conversations about race, which were frequently diminished to cherry-picking cultural holidays or foods before returning to white as usual. Substantial effort from families who have adopted white racial framing ensured that race was only discussed in superficial and discounting ways at best, disregarded entirely, or even blatantly anti-Black or anti-Asian.

CHAPTER 8

White Women

Oppression Olympics, White Saviors, and Controlling Images

Not all perpetrators of microaggressions were considered of equal weight for respondents. Both Black and Asian American women reported that microaggression experiences were especially distinct when the aggressor was a white woman. Just as Black and Asian American women's lived experiences are shaped by their race and gender, white women's lives are also raced and gendered.[1] The intersection of their privileged race and simultaneously oppressed gender situates white women at a unique social location in society: as both oppressor and oppressed.

The reputation of white women as relentless microaggressors was shared across Black and Asian American women. When I first asked about white women in our interviews, I was consistently met with groans, laughs, and exaggerated sighs, followed by eagerness to talk about the microaggressions experienced at the hands of white women. In fact, no other code had more individual incidents than "white women" in my data analysis. These microaggressions spanned from the workplace to the grocery store; from strangers to best friends; from comments about clothing to language to men. Of all microaggressive perpetrators that my respondents discussed, white women seemed to be the most expected but also to cause the most distress. Kamara is a Black, straight, twenty-nine-year-old graduate student. Having grown up outside of San Diego, she attended schools with some racial diversity but limited Black students before moving to the East Coast to study ecology. She is one of few students of color in her graduate program. During our interview, Kamara shared she felt "least comfortable around white women," noting this unease was specifically due to their location as oppressor/oppressed: "I totally feel like it's a different kind of racism because some of them think that they're kind of immune [to racism] because they're women. So they'll say things, you know, saying things about Black men. They think because they're talking about a man that I'm going to agree."

The assumption of such "sisterhood" is not new. Audre Lorde, bell hooks, Mikki Kendell, and many other women of color have written extensively about the problem that is white women's presumptions of sisterhood as an excuse to be racist.[2] The unique social location of white women as oppressor/oppressed allows them to act as advocates for white domination but through a back door approach that softens the motive; sisterhood, after all, implies that we look out for one another when faced with oppressive forces. Yet through Oppression Olympics, white saviorism, and a rigid subscription to controlling images of women of color, white women demonstrated their commitment to upholding the white domination from which they benefit through everyday racist encounters with Black and Asian American respondents.

The Oppression Olympics and the Damsel in Distress

As Sunnie's sister demonstrated in the prior chapter, women of color are no stranger to navigating white women's adoption of Oppression Olympics. Oppression Olympics refer to a practice of one-upping victimhood, which serves to discredit or minimize the subjugation of a group that is marginalized at multiple axes.[3] Of course, all marginalized identities do share one thing in common: their oppression under inequitable social forces. However, the liberation of those with multiple marginalized identities cannot be essentialized; women's liberation, as a general struggle for social change, does not necessarily reflect the needs of all women within the overarching group.[4] When white women use gendered racist microaggressions to employ Oppression Olympics, they imply that the racist sexism women of color experience as both gender and racially marginalized identities is not significantly unique from the sexism that white women experience in a patriarchal system of power.

Why is victimhood so appealing that it seems to warrant a competition? On the surface, those who engage in Oppression Olympics perhaps compete for who has it worse to argue that the empathy, policy solutions, or other attention one marginalized group may receive is undeserving in relation to their own subordination. However, I posit there are two deeper motives. First, when employed by white women, Oppression Olympics can be used as a tactic to normalize everyday racism and recenter whiteness. Second and relatedly, Oppression Olympics also protect white women from being labeled as Racist-with-a-capital-R. By distracting from, minimizing, or outright denying the significance of racism on everyday oppression for women of color, white women view themselves as comrades in the struggle against (white) patriarchy rather than coconspirators in the maintenance of white supremacy. To an Oppression Olympics athlete, these roles are mutually exclusive. Rather than the all-too-commonly uttered excuse for accountability—"I can't be racist; I have Black friends!"—white women are instead able to claim, "I can't be racist; I am also oppressed!"

That is not to say that everyday gender and racial acts of oppression hold no similarities between them. Philomena Essed acknowledged the commonalities between gender and racial discriminations, including being talked down to, being tokenized, and being subordinate in favor of white men. Pierce, too, likened perpetrators of sexism to perpetrators of racism.[5] The differences, then, cannot be overlooked; whites avoid contact with people of color as a form of everyday racism, yet the opposite form, uninvited physical contact, is an everyday act against women.[6] The problem with such analogizing, according to Essed, is that women of color become invisibilized here. Are they avoided as nonwhites, or unconsensually touched as women? The answer, of course, is both. Without understanding the "separate as well as mutually interwoven formations of race and gender," we cannot account for the ways in which women of color experience everyday gendered racism, shaped by white supremacist patriarchy that adapts and evolves in contradictory ways to always remain in domination.[7]

Intersectionality scholar Ange-Marie Hancock outlines five tenets of Oppression Olympic ideology.[8] For the relevancy of this research, I define each tenet within racialized and gendered frameworks, although other marginalized identities including sexuality, class, disability, nationality, and age may also be weaponized or subjugated under Oppression Olympics. The first tenet, *leapfrog paranoia*, describes a "me first" approach to Oppression Olympics that embodies their competitive nature. As a historical example, consider evidence of leapfrog paranoia in the suffragette movement as white American women's political platform was rooted in the argument that they should gain voting rights before Black (male) Americans.[9] *Willful blindness* describes a deliberate ignorance of one's own political agency in order to cast oneself in pure victimhood. For example, by ignoring the privilege and power of their own whiteness, white women can claim that their subjugation under patriarchy is the worst form of social oppression. Next, *movement backlash* occurs when groups with one or more privileged identities believe that progress of the oppressed infringes on their own rights and agency. Once again, early white feminist suffragettes set quite a textbook example for movement backlash, when Susan B. Anthony declared she would "cut off her right arm" before she advocated for the rights of Black voters over women voters.[10] The continuation of this us-versus-them mentality persists today, with claims that the celebration of the Black Lives Matter movement or affirmative action policies are "reverse racism." This zero-sum presumption implies that Black liberation is only possible at the expense of (white) women. Next, *defiant ignorance* describes the denial of stratified power systems and all oppression that occurs beneath them. For example, white women may avoid learning about housing discrimination practices in their neighborhoods if those practices do not directly affect their own opportunities for homeownership, to absolve themselves of accountability or guilt. Finally, *compassion deficit disorder* describes a misplaced or absent sense of compassion, and a victim-blaming ideology that dehumanizes the oppressed. For example, one may feel compassion for an accused sexual assaulter rather than that assaulter's victims.[11]

Each of these tenets relies on color blindness to discount how women of color are subjugated at multiple axes, and as such, at the crux of Oppression Olympics is a disregard for intersectionality. In her open letter to author Mary Daly, feminist lesbian writer Audre Lorde writes, "The oppression of women knows no ethnic nor racial boundaries, true, but that does not mean it is identical within those differences."[12] A few years later, she reiterates this sentiment in her popular essay *The Use of Anger*, noting, "I am not free while any woman is unfree, even when her shackles are very different from my own." [13] Quite stark in comparison to Susan B. Anthony's contentious quote above, Lorde acknowledges that women do not suffer identical oppressions in patriarchy, but our liberation is still a communal struggle. A woman's race, class, age, nationality, sexuality, and ability and how those identities interact with gender all dictate how patriarchy reads a person, benefits them, or kills them. Yes, all women share the experience of oppression under a patriarchal system, but the tightness of those shackles, the coldness, the strength of the materials used in their construction, and our historical and societal relationship with who holds the keys to those shackles are not identical. Acknowledging these differences allows us to understand the nuance of power and oppression and still does not negate the impact of the imprisonment; we do not need to "win" at whose shackles are worse, and we do not need to be socially located at every margin to advocate for those who are.

Yet, Oppression Olympics allow white women to neglect the relevance of such different shackles on how sexism is experienced through color blindness. Color blindness hinges on an adoption of neoliberalism that does not acknowledge race as an obstacle or advantage to success.[14] When white women claim they "do not see race"—a microaggression in and of itself—women of color's experiences with oppression are then reduced to their other clearly marginalized identity: gender. Minimizing the significance that race has on women of color's lives creates an opportunity for white women to claim equal footing with women of color in a skewed and oversimplified understanding of power and privilege. Color blindness thus allows white women to engage comfortably in Oppression Olympics, as the power afforded to them by their whiteness is masked by their marginalization under patriarchy.

Many of my respondents recognized the ways in which white women employ Oppression Olympics through gendered racist microaggressions, pointing to the visibility of whiteness after all. Sunnie describes Oppression Olympics as a practice she experienced not only with her sister but specific to white women in general:

> I do not like it when white women try to compete with women of color like, "Oh, we are more marginalized." I don't think that that's healthy. I don't think that it's good to create a hierarchy. So I don't try to do that. But you do face women of color who are saying, "No, this is a specifically racialized attack or microaggression towards me or towards whoever," and white women are like, "Well, you know, we're also marginalized too, because we're women." And it's like, well, this is not a competition! And I don't see that so much coming from women of color. I don't see women of color, or even women of color who are LGBTQ, taking these parts of their identity, and I guess you could say weaponizing them where we're battling each other. And it's my perception, at least my experience, that white women do that. Maybe it's because, as white people, they do have a lot of privileges. So there is maybe either a cognitive dissonance or this inner conflict. . . . I don't know what it is that they need to work out, but they need to work that out (laughs).

An intersectional theoretical perspective recognizes that women of color experience a unique oppression due to the intersection of their race and gender.[15] The sexism that women of color experience in a patriarchal society is wrapped up and inseparable from the racism they also experience in a white supremacist one: an experience that white women are not familiar with. White women's whiteness protects them from being perceived as out of place in white space. But furthermore, white women's whiteness affords them the privileges that come with adjacency to white men. This situates white women at a unique place within structures of domination and power as well, as they occupy both oppressor and oppressed. White women are not unfamiliar with patriarchal oppression; however, a familiarity with sexism cannot be accurately extended to experiences of oppression outside of that identity.

When discounting the significance of race to Black and Asian American women, white women engage in willful blindness. Even white women who share other historically oppressed identities, such as being low income or queer, are capable of weaponizing color blindness. White women's reputation as engagers of color-blind microaggressions through Oppression Olympics was largely presumed by both Asian American and Black respondents. Andrea, a Black queer woman who recently left her job at a predominantly white university, discusses the way her boss, a queer white woman, utilized both willful blindness and defiant ignorance to engage in Oppression Olympics:

> What I found a lot with the white woman that was my boss is that it literally was like, yes, we can talk about women's things and sometimes queer things, but anytime it became race it was just not a thing she could do, not a thing that she could hear. She did not believe that she was perpetrating oppression in that way. She literally did not believe that. And it was really hard to work for someone who saw themselves as really social justice focused, really understanding intersectionality, and can speak the language for miles but never actually looked at herself. And it has been my experience, especially with queer women, that I just avoid them because they have enough language to be dangerous.

Andrea viewed the racial protection that white women have, regardless of other marginalized identities, as dangerous, especially from white women who can "speak the language" of critically analyzing oppressive systems. This particular white woman was familiar with the powerful social forces enough to critique unequal systems that sustain her own subordination but was unable to be held accountable—to "look at herself"—for her own power and agency over racially oppressed women.

Historically, white women have weaponized their privilege to maintain white domination at the expense of people of color. This is only possible through white women's proximation to white men. White women have held positions of power in white supremacist organizations,[16] owned enslaved peoples,[17] and made countless accusations of violence that cost innocent Black men their lives (e.g., Emmett Till, the Scottsboro Boys, the Exonerated Five, and Christopher Cooper). White women's own racialized femininity affords them the myth of pure white womanhood, an identity that is protected by white men.[18] Ruby Hamad refers to "damsel in distress" behavior from white women that ensures their power yielded through whiteness is concealed by the virtue, innocence, and subordination that is attributed to white womanhood. Hamad notes, "The damsel ensured that white women were at least considered human, even though it came at the cost of relegating them to subordinate status. But it did so by ruthlessly excluding nonwhite women from the construction of womanhood."[19] This allows white women to work behind the scenes in support of white supremacist maintenance all while nodding in apparent solidarity with women of color as fellow women. Andrea's white, queer boss was undoubtedly no stranger to sexist and homophobic prejudices, and those experiences cannot be discounted. But her inability to understand race as a shackle different from her own invoked a denial of Andrea's experiences by weaponizing color blindness alongside her critical knowledge of queer and gender subjugation.

When use of Oppression Olympics, color blindness, or meritocracy is challenged, white women can evoke damsel in distress behavior to deflect the significance of race once again. Sailem, a Black, queer, college student in her early twenties, recalls a class discussion with a white woman classmate regarding white privilege. Her classmate's white partner was chosen for a job over his Black friend despite the friend's higher GPA. The classmate attributed her partner's success to an unpaid internship he completed that made him more qualified for the position, arguing that privilege was unrelated to him obtaining the job. Sailem argues that privilege still played a role:

> I'm like, "Yeah, okay, so what you're saying right now is, because your boyfriend's friend did not do free labor, he didn't get the job.... Do you not see the privilege?" And then she's mad. She is really mad and she starts yelling. Mind you, she's *yelling*! And then she goes, "I'm not privileged—I was raped! Yeah, I got married really young, my husband was abusive, and I left him. I don't have my parents paying for me to go to school!" And she's crying. Proceed tears. "My parents don't have money. My parents don't pay!" And I'm speaking this tone the whole time. I'm like, "Yeah I hear you, but none of our parents are paying for us to go to school either." The professor tells me to stop yelling at her.

Richard Dyer claims that whites set the standard of humanity in ways that benefit their own success.[20] Such standards are embodied within a white racial frame, where white norms are considered universal societal norms as well. Crying, as a societal norm, communicates injury and helplessness, which elicits automatic sympathy for Sailem's classmate. Her helplessness was legitimized through her tears, which also absolved her of accountability for the initial color-blind microaggressive offense.[21] Conversely, Sailem, whose behavior (and Blackness) did not fall within the standard of white societal victimhood, was blamed by the white, male professor for causing distress to her classmate.

The weaponizing of tears is strategic: crying and other symbols of distress can re-empower white women who have been challenged with the label of Racist-with-a-capital-R, especially in the presence of white men. Just ask Jennifer Schulte, a white woman known more commonly as "BBQ Becky," who, in the spring of 2018, called police on a Black family barbecuing at a public California park. When the police arrived two hours after the initial call, Schulte broke down in tears, heaving sobs of "I am being harassed!" while the responding officer (a white man) instructs the Black woman recording the incident to "back off."[22] It is obvious who is perceived as aggressor and victim to the officer, regardless of who initiated harassment.

Femininity and masculinity are raced and coconstructed in relation to each other.[23] Hamad argues that the damsel in distress paradigm is clear verification of such: "The damsel in distress reveals that from the beginnings of settler-colonial societies, race was gendered and gender was raced. Only white men were Man and only white women were Woman."[24] Although rarely spoken outright, we see evidence of this belief all around us. Controlling imagery of Black women depict them as angry, hyper- or desexualized, and unqualified for feminine-aligned expectations of motherhood, respectable marriage, or humanity at all. Likewise, controlling imagery of Asian women casts them as worthy of such feminine roles *only* when those duties benefit white men. The goalposts of womanhood and femininity change depending on who is trying to claim it. Vanesia, a Nigerian American, twenty-year-old college student, explains, "The concept of womanhood is so frustrating to me because there's the Angry Black Woman stereotype, but anger is masculine. So Black women are ostracized from womanhood because womanhood and fragility are tied to each other. So womanhood is white. That's just saying Black women can't really be women."

The classmate's employment of Oppression Olympics embodies willful blindness. She denied the reality of anti-Black hiring practices, as well as her own white privilege, and redirected the victimization to herself as a survivor of sexual assault. Of course, the classmate's sexual assault was not related to the reason her partner was hired over his Black friend. Nor was it related to who paid her college tuition. Yet, her ability to weaponize tears when her color blindness is challenged ensures that she will not be construed as Racist-with-a-capital-R. Paired with the professor's microaggression instructing Sailem to "stop yelling" when using an even tone, Sailem knows that within a white racial frame that promotes white societal norms, regardless of who was yelling she would be cast as the aggressor. Irrespective of this woman's subjugated gender and identity as a survivor of sexual assault, hers and other white women's tears are fundamental to the maintenance of white supremacy.[25] Oppression Olympics allow the ramifications of racism to be disregarded while the damsel in distress trope ensures its invisibility goes unchallenged.

"I'm Not Poor; I'm Just Black!"

CONTROLLING IMAGES AND WHITE SAVIORISM

Sailem's classroom experience reveals the continued influence of controlling imagery. Despite using a conversational tone, she was cast as the aggressor—the angry

Black woman—attacking her innocent classmate. Controlling images are widespread stereotypes that simultaneously preserve, deny, and justify the oppression of women of color.[26] Angry Black women, hypersexual Jezebels, welfare queens, submissive Lotus Blossoms, and scheming dragon ladies all reflect racialized, gendered controlling imagery of Black and Asian women, stereotypes of which are still adopted and embraced today. The espousal of these stereotypes guarantees that the consequences of white patriarchal supremacy on Black and Asian women are blamed on their own presumed behavior rather than on sociohistorical, macrolevel disinvestment and inequalities. By reducing individual people to monolithic caricatures, women of color are robbed of their individuality—a privilege reserved for whiteness.

White women subscribe to controlling images of Black and Asian women to promote and maintain white supremacist patriarchy and communicate this rigid view through gendered racist microaggressions. At times, Black women respondents identified white women as heavy subscribers to all controlling images outlined by Patricia Hill Collins, but one in particular was popular among white women: the poor Black woman. The poor Black woman, or welfare mother, attests to how gender and race are classed as well. This trope legitimizes the disinvestment in Black families and communities by casting Black women as lazy, unwilling to work, and abusing government subsidies. Never mind the fact that Black women are more often discriminated against in job interviews,[27] tracked into low-paying service work,[28] and paid less once they get hired.[29] No, the poor Black woman trope negates these data to rationalize Black poverty as the fault of careless individual choices.

Respondents received messages from white women through gendered racist microaggressions that communicated Black women are inherently poor, uneducated, and perpetually reliant on government assistance. Alicia is a twenty-eight-year-old, straight Black woman pursuing a PhD. Although her graduate program paid her a stipend and tuition (a common funding arrangement in social science graduate programs), Alicia worked weekends as a server at a senior living facility to supplement her pay. She describes a conversation she had with one white woman in the care of the facility:

> This one older white woman had taken a liking to me, which is fine. I ended up opening up by telling her that I was getting my doctorate. She was like, "Oh, our, our son is in so-and-so he's getting his doctorate! He's going to be an oncologist; he's going to be a doctor!" Then she starts asking me how I pay for school. I was like, well, I got a fellowship and everything else. "Oh, how'd you get that? Is it from the government?" And I was like, "Um, well, no. But, um, you know, I'm just going to go, I have other tables."

Academic fellowships to pursue graduate degrees come in all shapes and sizes—from the department itself, the larger university, or public and private research agencies. Yet, the controlling image of the poor Black woman living off government funds is so ingrained within a white racial framework that this white woman was unable to imagine any reality for Alicia beyond government assistance. She never volunteered information about her son's ability to afford tuition, yet felt entitled to question Alicia on hers. This entitlement further alludes to her adoption of another controlling image—the mammy—in which a power imbalance entitles white women to interrogate their Black female servants on their personal lives. Shannon Sullivan's theory of *ontological expansiveness* applies here; whites' perceived entitlement to space includes control over environments in which there is an alleged superior-dominated relationship.[30] The mammy is obedient, subordinate, and faithful to the white family she serves, and thus when she is asked a question, she is happy to answer; the white lady of the house is entitled to know such information, after all. With a rigid subscription to controlling images of Black women, this white woman expected no different from Alicia.

As white women occupy a sociopolitical position of oppressor/oppressed, they can adopt simultaneous identities of both victim and savior. This provokes a white savior industrial complex in which white knowledge is considered necessary to save those less privileged, without consideration of the policies and systems whites have promoted that reinforce that same inequality.[31] Through an intersectional lens, white saviorism is not only contingent on whiteness, but it is also gendered and classed. Hamad details the gendered aspects of white saviorism: "The language of the white savior is not one of liberation or sisterhood: it is a language of imperialism. Nothing gives away a White Savior Complex like white women rallying to 'save' brown women despite the gruesome history of what 'saving' has entailed."[32]

White women perceive Black women as in need of saving from the ills of Black womanhood, which controlling imagery ensures is conflated with poverty. Because controlling images serve to blame individuals rather than systems, Black women are (1) often assumed to be poor and (2) assumed to be poor *because of* bad personal choices they made. These assumptions not only distract from the influence of systemic disinvestment and white supremacist patriarchy on Black women's lives but further provides an opportunity for white women to save the day. At best (and admittedly, at a stretch), white saviorist behaviors may generate interest convergence, wherein both parties seemingly benefit. But more likely, white saviorism exists to serve whites who are "able to be emotionally rewarded about the contribution made to the cause and that he or she has made a difference in the lives of these poor unfortunate individuals," while also *causing harm* to the very people they are alleged to be helping.[33]

But what better way to be shielded from the label of Racist-with-a-capital-R than to be a superficial saving grace for Black women? Briana, a thirty-two-year-old queer Black woman living in Georgia, recounts an exchange with a white woman coworker from her time at the Department of Transportation: "So, one of the ladies in the department that I worked in, she was like, 'I'm getting rid of some of my daughter's clothes and some jackets and stuff. You know, do you want to look at them?' I'm like, 'Yeah, sure.' And she's like, 'Yeah, I know, it'd be like a second Christmas for you!' And I'm just like . . . 'What? I'm not poor; I'm just Black!'"

Briana accepted her coworker's offer for secondhand clothes initially believing it to be a simple friendly gesture but soon realized the white woman viewed her as poor and in need of free clothing as charity. The coworker's assumption that receiving her daughter's used clothes was the equivalent to Christmas gifts reflects her adoption of the poor Black woman controlling imagery. Briana, who admits she has more clothes than she needs, laughs at the memory: "She really thought she was doing me a favor."

White women's commitment to endorsing this stereotype, when paired with an adoption of a white savior complex, gives rise to gendered racist microaggressions that my respondents felt were particularly offensive. The enactors of such comments varied by age, sexual orientation, and relationship to my respondents, but one thing they each had in common was that they were all white women. Ciara, a Black, straight, graduate student studying public health, was subjected to many white women coworkers and classmates who adopted the poor Black woman controlling images and white saviorism through work in disadvantaged, often Black, communities in metro Atlanta. She lamented, "All Black people are not people that need your help!" White saviorist microaggressions convey that Black women and communities are poor, unable to help themselves, and in need of charity work that only white people are capable of bestowing.

In defining microaggressions, Pierce provides examples of five offensive mechanisms by which microaggressions operate. He describes the first example as, "We love you Blacks to death," which characterizes both a white saviorist perpetrator and a target that must demonstrate appreciation for the savior. After all, the primary purpose of the "saving" is the recognition and praise. In another example, "You Blacks are sick," perpetrators assert their power through whiteness to be saviors of perceived Black misfortune in the first place. Pierce explains, "At the end of the offensive action, the black feels and perceives that the white has communicated: 'You Blacks are so sick that we must use all our power to protect you for your own sake.' . . . He is told that he doesn't understand his problem because he is too distorted in his outlook."[34]

It is through both the assertion of power and the expectation of recognition that white saviorism becomes routine and obligatory to white women. Although Pierce's original inception of microaggressions as offensive mechanisms were specifically describing experiences of Black Americans, the collective message points to the reaffirmation of racial superiority of whites above all nonwhites.[35] We cannot forget that the function of microaggressions is not solely about the interaction between two people inasmuch as how that interaction confirms and endorses white supremacy more generally.

Asian American women also experienced microaggressions from white women that demonstrated their adoption of controlling images and validate presumed white superiority. Rather than angry and poor, white women fostered controlling imagery of Asian American women as Lotus Blossoms. The Lotus Blossom controlling image—sometimes called the China doll—dominates characterizations of East Asian women. She is submissive, obedient, pleasant, and aims to please her white American husband. And perhaps above all else, the Lotus Blossom represents both the mystery of the exotic Orient and of whites' conquering of it.[36] Her submissiveness epitomizes her Eastern upbringing; that is precisely what makes her perpetually foreign and unaccultured to the West.

Previous research on Asian American experiences of microaggressions outline perpetually foreign messages for all Asian Americans.[37] However, much of the research that has established this as a common theme among Asian Americans has predominantly analyzed Asian American women, yet do not frame the experiences intersectionally. For example, Derald Wing Sue and colleagues' 2007 work revealing common themes of Asian American microaggressions included a total of ten (n = 10) Asian American participants, nine of whom were women. The adoption of controlling imagery evident in their findings (such as *exotification of Asian American women*) further point to gender differences in how microaggressions are used against Asian Americans. Controlling imagery is heavily dependent on gender: Asian women are stereotyped quite differently from Asian men, especially in regard to sexuality.[38] Accordingly, I argue microaggressions that convey a rigid adoption of controlling imagery are both raced and gendered.

Rarely, if ever, mentioned in modern microaggression research is what Pierce termed the "pat and promise" offense. Nestled under the description "We love you Blacks to death," this offense ensures the target of a microaggression feels "that the good faith registered by white solicitude is sufficient."[39] Although I found only one other paper that discusses the pat and promise by name (a dissertation written by one of Pierce's graduate students, no less),[40] modern microaggression research alludes to its essence often. The pat and promise is all about intent. First, it protects whites who "have Black friends," read anti-racism books, and voted for Barack Obama (twice!) from being labeled as Racist-with-a-capital-R. But furthermore, the pat and promise allows offenders to defend their microaggressive comments under an excuse of intent. Recall Serena's experience at her brother's birthday party: her mother insisted the visiting white family was not racist because their *intention* was not to harm Serena with their bewilderment at her presence in a white household. However, the effect on Serena was not swayed by the family's intention. Yet, oppression does not require intent to operate; it requires compliance. The microaggression communicated that Serena did not belong in white space, irrespective of intent.

When white women demonstrated a rigid subscription to controlling imagery, Asian American respondents seemed to focus on intent more so than Black women respondents. Asian American women regarded white women's intentions as mostly innocuous, or at least not outwardly malicious. Given the racial triangulation of Asian Americans, this is less perplexing than it may appear. Consider the "honorary white" status of many (primarily East) Asian Americans: a dubious identity imposed on light-skinned people of color by whites.[41] The purpose of this middle positioning is twofold: first, it serves to create tensions between Asian Americans and other people of color by reinforcing a racial hierarchy that places whiteness at the top and Blackness at the bottom. Additionally, it creates a false promise for Asians and other alleged "honorary whites" that they, too, will have access to the benefits of whiteness (and be even further distanced from the burden of Blackness) if they adapt to and promote the hierarchy.[42] Of course, the perpetually foreign controlling imagery ensures that Asians will never be seen as white, and the few privileges of whiteness that seemingly can be gained by Asians are unstable and fleeting, as the COVID-19 pandemic so clearly demonstrated. However, the false promise of attaining such white privileges conveys to Asian Americans that protecting whiteness is a practice in future self-preservation.

Asian American women were not necessarily less bothered by everyday racism than Black women respondents; their sighs, tears, and frustrated voices when recalling these accounts illustrates that. Yet, the tendency to rescue white women from their racist behavior through qualifying a perpetrator's intention demonstrates the pervasiveness of the white racial frame. Such tears and frustration attest to the futility of intent—the harm lies within the racialized Othering. White women's assumptions that Asian American women are more adoptive of their ethnicities' cultures than the American culture in which most of them were raised is contingent on forever foreign controlling imagery; white Americans with Irish, German, or Nordic ancestry are rarely assumed to be immersed in their ancestral cultural practices the way Asian Americans are. This reaffirms the very racialized Othering that sustains forever foreign ideologies about Asian Americans, regardless of however many generations their families have lived in the United States, whether they speak their heritage language, or even, like Sunnie, if they grow up as the sole person of color in an otherwise all-white household. Danielle, a queer Chinese American geologist, qualifies intent as she explains, "People from the kindness of their hearts and with good intentions want to know or share facts about my culture. I am so separated from my culture; I don't even speak Chinese!" When I asked for an example, Danielle describes her white woman therapist's small gestures as well-intended but off-putting:

> She tries so hard to be inclusive and learn about my culture because I am probably her only Asian client. Almost every session she will have some little tidbit or some fact she learned about. It's kind of sweet, but I'm also like, how do I tell this person that this is annoying to me? . . . Last week, there was a book written by a Chinese American woman who talks about how it was hard for her to grow up Chinese American because of all these gender pressures and things. And to be fair, it was very relevant to what we were talking about, but it rubbed me the wrong way. Stuff like that. I would wear a red shirt and she would say, "Oh, that's a lucky color in your culture!"

Danielle's therapist likely thought she was utilizing culturally competent practices by incorporating Chinese books and references into their sessions. However, Danielle's culture is not exclusively Chinese, even if her ethnicity is. This distinction is often disregarded, if recognized at all, for Asian American women, a reminder of the unattainability of being American.

Microaggressions that communicate a subscription to Asian Americans as foreigners reify whiteness as the American standard and whites as the power holders to set that standard. We don't know what happens behind closed doors; perhaps Danielle's therapist also attributes her white clients' clothing to American cultural significance (red is also on the U.S. flag, after all). But to Danielle, these seemingly harmless gestures only othered and tokenized her to a monolithic Chinese woman's experience. It was not the book itself that bothered Danielle but rather the message that conveyed she must relate to it solely due to her Chinese identity. Even when the materials were significant to their session, the repeated cumulation of microaggressions from her white therapist felt like an overcorrection of color blindness into tokenism.

Color blindness is used to absolve people of guilt and/or accountability for racism; if someone "does not see race," they can convince themselves they are incapable of enacting or upholding racialized inequalities.[43] Recently, as systemic racism becomes a topic more widely discussed beyond the confines of academia, the adoption of color blindness has been more often recognized as problematic. Public programming, employers, and professional graduate programs promote cultural competency strategies and trainings to emphasize that diversity matters. However, this can lead to an overcorrection of color blindness that results in tokenism. Undoubtedly, Danielle's life experiences are influenced by her identity as a Chinese woman but also of her life as entirely situated within the United States. Her therapist's overcorrection of color blindness implied that Danielle's life centered on being Chinese, when sometimes a red shirt is just a red shirt.

Although Asians have been present in the United States for centuries, controlling imagery characterizes all Asians as recent migrants, unacculturated to U.S. customs, language, and food. White women even imposed this stereotype on children. For example, when Clara, a biracial Vietnamese woman, was in second grade, her white teacher recommended she attend English speakers of other language (ESOL) classes. ESOL classes are for students whose first language is not English. Recall that Clara was born and raised in a small suburb of Atlanta with a white father and Vietnamese mother. English is, in fact, her first language. She shares, "The only reason they put me in that class was because my mom came to the school. She speaks English well, but it's not perfect. But they put me in ESOL because she wasn't fluent in English. And yeah. So for the first half of the year, I missed recess every single day because I would go to ESOL."

Within a white racial frame, Asians and Asian Americans are depicted as poor English speakers, their speech and language mocked as part of a forever foreign controlling imagery, framing Asian Americans (and other people of color) as culturally inferior.[44] Accents associated with nonwhite skin, such as Asian, Latinx, or Black accents, are subjected to racialized mocking or assumptions of inferior intelligence in ways that European accents are not.[45] Clara's teacher assumed her Vietnamese mother's imperfect English reflected Clara's own fluency in the language. At seven years old, Clara did not question where teachers instructed her to go. We must recognize the power dynamic present here in which recognizing and resisting microaggressions may not always be feasible. Instead of challenging her teacher, she went to ESOL classes for months. Interestingly, neither the ESOL teacher nor Clara's general studies teacher realized this mistake despite the months she attended; Clara's Asian appearance, paired with a single event in which her mother was observed speaking less-than-perfect English, solidified to both parties that Clara must not be fluent in her own first language.

Schools served as a common location of gendered racist microaggressions throughout my respondents' lives. Existing research has largely focused on microaggression experiences in colleges, but my findings suggest grade schools are also rampant sites of everyday racism from both peers and teachers. This is especially important to consider in terms of power when teachers microaggress their students. Sarah is a Korean, Chinese, and white thirty-one-year-old woman who grew up in the suburbs of Washington, D.C. She identifies as fourth generation, as she is a descendent of Chinese migrants who came to the United States to build railroads in the late nineteenth century. Sarah shares an incident that occurred in middle school when a substitute teacher, a white woman, asked the students to share where their families were from:

> So my white classmates are going around and being like, "Oh, I'm a quarter Portuguese and Italian and German and English," you know, all of this stuff. Then we got to me, and I told her, "Oh, my family's from California originally, and I'm part Chinese and Korean." And for some reason, even though she said "cool" after the white and other people saying all of the things that they were, for some reason for me, she was like, "Oh, you're like one of those mutts, aren't you?" and then proceeded to go on a deep dive of like, "Okay, so you're not really from California, then?" and I'm like, at least as far back as all of these other white people, but for some reason, you know, the answer I gave just wasn't enough.

This white substitute teacher subscribed to the controlling image of the perpetually foreign Asian and microaggressed Sarah by refusing to accept that her family was "really from California." Yet, while her classmates shared German, Italian, and Portuguese ethnic ties, their belonging in the United States went unchallenged. Furthermore, the substitute derogatorily equated Sarah's multiracial ethnicity to a mixed-breed dog, recalling a long history of the literal dehumanization of nonwhite women. When I asked Sarah if she pushed back in response to the substitute's interrogation, she alluded to the power dynamics that inevitably exist within teacher-student spaces. She recalls, "I was twelve. But even at that age, I was like, that is definitely a word she did not use for other people. And this line of questioning is weirdly invasive. But I didn't really say anything because you know, it was an authority figure, right?" But the power dynamic is more than just that of teacher-student or adult-child; whites hold the social power to gatekeep who is "American" over people of color.

Conclusion

Throughout my research, white women assumed their experiences with oppression were identical to racist oppressions as well. This mindset served to advance and excuse their perpetration of gendered racist microaggressions. White women microaggressed both Black and Asian American women in similar and distinct ways that ultimately demonstrate color blindness, Oppression Olympics, and a rigid adoption of controlling imagery to uphold their investment in white supremacy. This rigidity ensures that regardless of whether Black or Asian American women debunk or confirm stereotypical traits, there is an eternal circulation of controlling images that ultimately sustains the domination of whiteness as justly earned and even necessary to save women of color from the ills of their nonwhite circumstance. Meanwhile, Black and Asian Americans are pushed to the margins as racialized Others, which characterizes them as unfamiliar with and undeserving of the norms of white America.

White women perpetrators elucidate the importance of an intersectional perspective; all victims of oppression are not victims of all oppressions. Despite being subordinated as women in a patriarchal society, their whiteness affords them power through their proximation to white men. A long history of weaponizing this power exists for white women, whose virtue, presumed innocence, and subservience to white men have defined the socially acceptable boundaries of femininity and who is allowed to claim it. At best, this earns white women the reputation that elicited the sighs, groans, and eye rolls that my respondents uttered when I first brought up white women as enactors of microaggressions; at worst, this costs people of color their dignity, their humanity, and their psychological and physiological health.

CHAPTER 9

White Sexual Imperialism and White Men

On Tuesday, March 16, 2021, a twenty-one-year-old white man walked into Big Woods Goods in Cherokee County, Georgia and purchased a 9MM handgun. Robert Aaron Long walked out of the firearms store and gun range with the weapon in hand, as there is no waiting period in the state of Georgia to purchase a firearm. He then traveled to Acworth, Georgia and waited for approximately one hour in the parking lot of Young's Asian Massage before entering the business. Long shot and killed two people at Young's, and two others later died at a hospital. Police arrived within minutes of his departure.[1]

Long then traveled roughly thirty miles to northeast Atlanta where he arrived at another Asian-owned business, Gold Massage Spa. Here, survivors report that the shooter was mostly silent during the attack except for stating, "I'm going to kill all Asians."[2] He locked the front and back doors of the business before shooting and killing three women.[3] Long then traveled across the street to Aromatherapy Spa, where he killed a final victim.

In total, eight people were shot and killed by Robert Aaron Long that afternoon. Of the eight victims, six were Asian women. Witnesses recalled that Long declared his plan to "kill all Asians" during the attack. He also admitted that his motive was fueled by a sexual addiction and that he viewed the women he targeted as "temptations." Despite those confessions, Cherokee County Sheriff's Office Captain Jay Baker later told media that the shooter was simply having "a really bad day" and that the murders were sexually but not racially motivated. Shortly thereafter, Baker himself was exposed for posting sinophobic material on his personal social media accounts.[4]

Racialized hate crimes of this magnitude are not what Philomena Essed was referring to when she described everyday racism. They are not what Chester Pierce had in mind when he wrote about microaggressions. But the relationship between such blatant racism and the mundane, everyday racism that Essed and Pierce studied cannot be ignored. They are two sides of the same coin that together justify white patriarchal supremacy at the expense of the lives of women of color. Robert Aaron Long saw Asian women as experiences rather than as individual people. He targeted businesses where he had received sexual services in the past, and each of the three businesses employed and/or were owned by Asian women. He frequented their services until he saw them as a threat to his self-control, and then he disposed of them in an irrevocable, violent way. Although his view of Asian women resulted in a murderous spree, his ideologies surrounding Asian women as sexual objects are not as rare as his actions. Both Asian American women and Black women respondents alike shared stories of white men perceiving them as sexual objects to be experienced. This common perception was communicated through gendered racist microaggressions in mundane, everyday interactions between my respondents and white men.

Gendered racist microaggressions from white men were primarily concentrated on this theme: Black and Asian American women are sexually distinct from white women. Orientalist exotification and Black hypersexualization are both contingent on controlling imagery. The Jezebel, or hoochie mama, is a Black woman with a sexual appetite that cannot be satiated. Her original purpose was to rationalize the rampant sexual assault by white men on Black enslaved women.[5] If Black women are so sexually promiscuous that they cannot be subdued, they ultimately cannot be victims of rape. The Jezebel controlling image continues to fulfill this purpose today: Black women are more likely to be sexually assaulted than white women during their lifetime but report those assaults far less often.[6] When they do report, they receive little support in return.[7] No wonder report rates are low.

For Asian women, we return to the controlling image of the Lotus Blossom. However, we now focus on the function of the Lotus Blossom for white men. As discussed in the prior chapter, the Lotus Blossom is hyperfeminine, hyperhetero, obedient, and forever foreign. But she is ultimately in servitude to her white male lover. She is so loyal to whiteness that she leaves behind her own country and the men within it to journey West as a bride to her new white husband. Like the Jezebel, the Lotus Blossom cannot be raped; her obedience masks as unwavering consent.[8] The Lotus Blossom's purpose is to "define the white men's virility and the white man's superiority."[9] She is different from white women because she is exotic, and that is what construes sex with Asian women—any Asian woman—as a unique experience for white men.

White Sexual Imperialism

Palestinian American political activist Edward Said describes *Orientalism* as a Western style of supremacy and domination over Asia and Asian diaspora.[10] Orientalism casts Asia and Asians as "the *other*" while the Western "Occident" remains the standard by which norms are set. The sexualization of Asian American women is rooted in the impression that Asian women are exotic and mystifying, elucidating the Otherizing of Orientalism. Immigration laws, Western imperialism in Asian countries, mail-order brides, and sex tourism reinforce this portrayal of Asian women as exotic sexual experiences.[11] In describing her theory of white sexual imperialism, legal scholar Sunny Woan points to the intersection of race and gender but also of belonging to a culture that has been impacted by Western imperialism as the underlying cause of inequity between white men and nonwhite women.[12]

Between the Philippine American War, World War II, the ongoing Korean War, and the Vietnam War, the United States has held a strong military presence all over Asia that shapes the way Asian women are viewed, including Asian diasporic women. Sex work around U.S. military bases is not uncommon but must be understood within a colonial context when those bases are located in Asian Pacific countries.[13] White racial framing follows U.S. service members even when overseas and constructs Asian societies as inferior to white Western societies and people. Documentation of sexual abuse, rape, and violence toward Asian women and girls—from sex workers to teenage students—by white service members in Asian Pacific countries demonstrates the dehumanization and often violent sexual objectification of Asian women by white men.[14] These women are regarded as existing solely to service white men, and thus their disposability after the job is complete becomes further justified. Perceptions of Asian women do not dissipate when servicemen return to the United States, though they alter slightly; white racial framing shapes controlling imagery that maintain such stereotypes for Asian American women as well. While the Asian sex worker in the East is sexually available to all white servicemen, once she travels to the United States with her new GI husband, she is available only to him: a domestic and loyal war bride.[15] History and modern research alike show that Asian American women have consistently been portrayed within a sexual light; the two most recognized controlling images of Asian women, the Lotus Blossom and the Dragon Lady, are superficially quite different, yet both highly defined by their sexual availability to white men.[16]

White Male Entitlement

At the crux of white sexual imperialism is white patriarchal entitlement. Western colonizers' long and widespread history of commandeering land, resources, and women in countries they are not native to demonstrates and further builds such entitlement. In the words of Ronald E. Hall, "It is this unjustified colonization experience that has sustained moral justifications of Western power even in the postcolonial era. . . . The result is a sense of entitlement that distorts their perceptions of fairness and impartiality. That entitlement has become a tradition among White males in particular, which denigrates any challenges to the Eurocentric status quo in America and elsewhere affected by its influence."[17]

Entitlement takes on many forms: from Robert Aaron Long's entitlement to take the lives of women he once used sexual services from, to the entitlement of white male slaveholders who raped and brutalized Black women, their bodies reduced to mere property to which their enslavers were, after all, legally entitled. In a society dominated by white supremacist patriarchy, white men's entitlement is presumed and justified through sociopolitical and economic power. The unjust enrichment of whites is achieved not by the pursuant of civil rights to which we are *all* entitled but through an assumption of entitlement based on historical investment, gendered racialized privilege, and subsequent power.

According to my respondents, white men felt entitled to women of color's bodies, time, affection, and personal information. Like their female counterparts, when white men asked respondents about personal details of their lives, they felt entitled to an answer without pushback. But entitlement was especially evident in white men's flirtations with Black and Asian women. Regardless of whether respondents were already partnered, genuinely uninterested, or even queer, they were on the receiving end of white men's entitlement. Nari is a queer Korean American woman in her mid-twenties living in Atlanta, Georgia. She recalls an incident at a bar when she was out with a few other queer Asian American women: "This white guy came up to us and said, 'Looks like I am going to be having dumplings for dinner tonight!' . . . I think because when I'm out, especially with people that identify as queer, we experience this form of . . . we experience a harsher form of fetishization. We aren't just fetishized for being Asian, but because men see us as couples, they are kind of like, 'looks like I am getting a two-for-one tonight.'"

Queer women are often fetishized by straight men who see their queerness as an obstacle of which they are entitled to challenge. Women's queerness is thus considered precarious, changeable, and fragile in contrast to natural, intrinsic heterosexuality. Heteronormativity is a macro social force that imposes straightness as instinctive and otherizes queerness. American poet and essayist Adrienne

Rich complicates this imposition in her essay *Compulsory Heterosexuality and Lesbian Existence*. Here, she expounds on the ways in which lesbian existence is neglected or invisibilized entirely; in its place, heterosexuality is deemed the default. The compulsory nature of heteronormativity speaks to its automatic and covert strategy. The tenuous assumption that queer women are open to engaging with straight men reflects how straight men adopt a compulsory heterosexuality ideology, perceive women's queerness as optional, and feel entitled to their time and attention.

The lewd comment toward Nari and her friends was gendered, racialized, and sexualized. The perpetrator assumed that because the women are queer, they would be willing to engage with each other, as well as him, simultaneously. He further assumed that because they are Asian American women, he was entitled to them as a straight white man. Finally, he refers to these women as dumplings, a food commonly associated with several East Asian cuisines. This comment is completely dependent not only on the identities of Nari and her friends as queer Asian American women but also his own as a straight, white man. The intersection of gender, race, and sexuality here was not lost on Nari. "When I get fetishized about that, like I said, it's not just because of my race or my gender but also because of my sexual orientation."

Such audacious comments cannot solely be blamed on the liquid courage of a complete stranger who had too much to drink at the bar. White men's entitlement is so pervasive that my respondents shared similar accounts even in professional environments. Briana, a Black woman in her early thirties who currently works at a dry cleaner, describes her recent interactions with a white male coworker: "He's always flirting, like 'Ooh, I'm about to take you to the back and we're gonna blah blah blah.' A joke like that. And it's like, 'Do you think because I'm Black that I would even consider . . . I'm just gonna fuck? Is that what this is?' I don't know what it is because I'm not giving anything off. I have a kid and you're married with kids. I'm not interested."

Briana confirmed that her coworker did not speak to other coworkers—all white women—in this manner. She believed these comments were directed at her exclusively because he saw her as the Jezebel: a hypersexual, untamed, promiscuous Black woman who is always available for sex.[18] His entitlement as a white man allowed him not only to bolster this controlling image but to "joke" with her about it on repeat occasions as well. Being in a workplace environment did not protect Briana, nor did being a mother herself, nor did her coworker's own status as married with children. Of course, women of all races are no stranger to sexual harassment in the workplace, yet we have to wonder why Briana's white coworkers were spared from this coworker's vulgar attention.

Asian Fetishization by White Men

There exists a predictable checklist of racialized pickup lines that arguably every Asian woman in the United States has heard at least once but more likely many, many times. Along with the *Full Metal Jacket* references that Sunnie recounted in a previous chapter, racialized and sexualized comments that exoticize and fetishize Asian American women have not changed much over the past several decades. Lizzie, a queer Korean American woman in her mid-twenties, sighs as she runs down a list of pickup lines she has heard from white men: "They would say, 'You look so different from other Asian girls.' They would ask, 'Where are you from? Where are you really from?' Then they would make comments like, 'You're so exotic' and those things. . . . 'Oh you're Korean? I love kimchi. I've dated a lot of Asian girls in my past.' Like, okay, why does that matter to me?"

These questions are predictable, banal, and border on intrusive, but they are also othering, exoticizing, gendered racist microaggressions. They interrogate Asian American women, assume heterosexuality, and diminish their cultural identities, once again, to food. They are more than mere questions one may ask a new acquaintance regardless of race because they reinforce white heteropatriarchal supremacy by reducing Asian women to monolithic sexual objects.

In particular, "Where are you really from?" is so frequently asked of Asian American women to communicate that they are perceived as exotic in white space. Over half of my Asian American respondents reported hearing this phrase used as a flirtatious line from straight white men. This common Orientalist question demonstrates the perpetrator's adoption of forever foreign controlling imagery and assumes that Asian American women are willing to share their ethnic background to strangers, further reflecting white entitlement to access. Although this phrase is often used as a pickup line, that is not its only function. Both Asian American and Black women received "where are you really from?" microaggressions from white men and white women who could not comprehend a reality in which women of color belong in a white-dominated America.

Lizzie felt white men would not tell white women about a history of dating other white women as a flirtation tactic, but to Asian American women, this microaggression implied an assumption of monoracial in-group trust; if one Asian woman gave this white man a chance, he is entitled to the trust of all Asian women! Lizzie was not the only Asian American respondent who learned of white men's dating record of Asian women. In some cases, the claim was used as a pickup line, and in others, Asian American women discovered their white partner's roster of Asian exes later on in relationships, raising suspicions of their own tokenization. Annie, a Chinese American community organizer in her early twenties, shares her experience with a white college boyfriend: "I couldn't get whether or not he was interested in me for who I was or for my ethnicity. And I ended up breaking up with him, and honestly, it was like a 30 to 40 percent reason why, because I just really couldn't figure it out. I knew that he had dated several Asian American women before me and I was just like, 'That's already giving me weird vibes; I don't know if you only date Asians, and I feel weird.'"

Annie shared that her white partner would often bring up "Asian-related topics" such as Japanese customs and Asian politics, which even furthered her suspicions and feelings of tokenization (recall that Annie claims Han Chinese ancestry, not Japanese). His interests, when paired with his history of dating primarily Asian women, led Annie to suspect that he fetishized Asian women. In her research on Asian American sexual politics, sociologist Rosalind Chou explains that for Asian American women, "it can be difficult to distinguish genuine interest from interest resting on fabricated constructions of an othered person. . . . The difficult part of interracial relationships for people of color is how to differentiate genuine interest from attraction based on preconceived notions."[19] Annie was unable to discern if her boyfriend *only* dated her because of an Asian fetish, but she also could not rule out that it was a possibility. Her skepticism reflects Miranda Fricker's notion of *hermeneutical injustice*, an inability to grasp one's own experience due to one's marginalization from the dominant framework.[20] In contrast to W. E. B. Du Bois's concept of double consciousness, hermeneutical injustice causes Annie to question the way the world experiences her as a racialized woman, rather than to understand her experiences through a veil. Pierce himself acknowledged similarly effective gaslighting from whites, operating through offensive mechanisms.[21] The uncertainty followed Annie through several years of dating other white men, unclear if their attention was rooted in ethnosexual stereotyping or a genuine interest in her as an individual person. "I remember thinking or feeling like I had it differently in a sense because I would always have to question why someone was into me, you know? Was it because of my Asianness?" Eliza, a Filipino woman in her early forties, shared similar skepticism of past partners who had mostly Asian exes. "If we were at the point in the relationship where we would learn about their previous partners, if they had only dated Asian women, it was always like, huh, maybe let's think about this. Which happened a lot. Like enough for me to notice that there is a slew of them."

If there was any doubt on the pervasiveness of controlling images, the popularity of Asian fetishization by white men should quell one's uncertainty. The fetishization of Asian women is a product of the white sexual imperialism that supports and maintains both Lotus Blossom and Dragon Lady controlling imagery as symbols of sexual conquest, obfuscating the way Asian women are perceived in their real lives. While Asian fetish microaggressions from white men may seem harmless on the surface, we must consider the foundation from which such comments occur. Western colonizers frequently used rape and sexual violence against colonized women as weapons of war.[22] At the intersection of white sexual imperialism and white male entitlement rests a dangerous justification for the violence that Asian women have experienced as a result of such fetishization.

The fetishization of Asian women is influenced by both a racialization of the body and racialization of sexuality. Asian women's bodies come in a variety of shapes and sizes, no different than other races; yet, Orientalism casts Asian women's bodies as foreign, unique, and exotic from non-Asians, implying that sex and the exploration of their bodies is also exotic, unique, and different from sex and exploration of a non-Asian body.

Bodies as Racialized Other

In 2017, an Asian American woman named Lillian created an account on the popular dating app Tinder. Noticing her encounters on the website were quite different from those of her white friends', she then created an Instagram account to highlight the messages she received from potential dates. The account, @thefleshlightchronicles, pairs photos of Lillian with screenshots of these messages, including gems such as "I'll eat your pussy like shrimp fried rice," "Do Asians really have tighter buttholes," and "Never been with an Asian before so banging you would be a dream come true. I need my yellow fever cured."[23]

Apparent in these comments, as well as in the accounts shared by Nari, Briana, and Lizzie above, the fetishization of women of color's bodies by white men is alive and well in practice.[24] Racialized fetishization implies that women of color are exotic and that sexual encounters with them are distinct from other (white) women. Accordingly, both Asian and Black women are perceived as exciting sexual experiences ("a dream come true") rather than as individual human beings, and microaggressions from white men reinforcing this view are incessant. My respondents heard such comments from strangers, from friends, from long-term partners, and from first dates. Sarah is a multiracial Korean, Chinese, and white woman in her early thirties. When she signed up for the dating app OkCupid, Sarah, like Lillian, was constantly subjected to racist sexualized messages from white men that implied her body was exotic and therefore access to it would be a unique and exciting experience. She described one incident that stuck with her: "I don't remember the exact wording, but I thought it was like, both white and Asian. And it was something about like, 'Which of your body parts are the Asian part?' or something, you know?" Yuna, a Korean American lawyer in her early forties, experienced similar body talk from white men at her college. "I remember in undergraduate years, they would be like, 'Oh, do you have a sideways vagina?' And I was like, I don't know what that is. I can assume no, I have a regular vagina."

Microaggressions alluding that Asian women's bodies are unlike white women's bodies are rooted in Orientalism and gendered racialized exotification, along with white racial framing defining white bodies as the norm. Exotification of non-white bodies depends on stereotyping sexual characteristics which further depicts women of color as the *other*, justifying the ethnosexual and systemic violence inflicted on them, including rape, invasion, or trafficking.[25] Consider, for example, the language that circulated in reports of Robert Aaron Long's attack; he viewed Asian women as sexual "temptations" that must be eliminated.[26] The temptress trope, after all, is not an innocent bystander in as much as a malicious seductress leading unsuspecting victims to betray their virtuous morals. Even in death, women of color are blamed for sexually tempting their own murderers.

Gendered racist exotification is only possible through comparison to a white norm. Through a rigid subscription of controlling imagery, Asian and Black women are cast as deviant from the norm of white women. However, the ways in which white womanhood is defined will vary depending on the function of its weaponization. When compared to the Black Jezebel, white women are characterized through feminine purity, virtuousness, and tame sexuality.[27] But when compared to the servile Lotus Blossom, white women are cast as liberation-seeking career women that have abandoned their virtue in pursuit of gender equity.[28] Once again, we cannot separate the context of U.S. imperialism from which controlling imagery of Asian women was constructed. Following the Korean and the Vietnam Wars, white American women sought liberation from patriarchy through "second wave" feminism, focusing on reproductive rights, sexual freedom, and domestic and workplace equity. Such demands challenged the patriarchal structure of which white men had historically defined the rules within institutions of families, workplaces, and medicine. Sunny Woan explains, "Believing American women to be too radical and career-oriented, many American men turned to mail-order bride companies for Asian wives who are 'loyal and undemanding.' Guided by sexual stereotypes of Asian women as subservient, these men saw Asian mail-order brides as the much-welcomed antithesis to the White American woman. Where the White feminist woman actively resisted subjugation, the Asian woman was portrayed as enjoying it."[29]

The comparison of white women to the Jezebel and the Lotus Blossom, though starkly different from each other, estrange women of color against white women to buttress the domination of patriarchal white supremacy. As usual, white men's desire is decidedly centered. In his study involving who straight white men were interested in dating, Wei-Chin Hwang found that 77.1 percent of white men surveyed were willing to date Asian women compared to 48.3 percent who were willing to date Black women.[30] The discrepancy between Asian American and Black women in relation to sexualization from white men can be traced to anti-Black ideologies in which Black women are devalued and portrayed as unattractive, masculine, animalistic, or angry. Of course, deemed worthy of marriage is not the same as deemed worthy to have sex with, especially when that sex has been constructed as an exciting and unique experience that bolsters white entitlement and power. Patricia Hill Collins argues that controlling images of Black women, including the Angry Black Woman and the Strong Black Woman, are at odds with the idealized notions of femininity.[31] Especially important here is the dehumanization of Black women that otherizes their bodies as nonhuman; while the fetishization of Asian women's bodies utilizes orientalism to explain her "exotic" body, Black women are seen as more "American" than Asian counterparts. Thus, the justification of their bodies as *other* is done through dehumanization to typecast them as markedly different from white bodies.

The most famous example of dehumanization of the Black woman's body is likely that of Sarah Baartman. Baartman was a Khoisan woman born in the late 1700s in the Western Cape of South Africa. She spent years of her life on display in London and Paris as an exhibit in "freak shows," brought to Europe by a Scottish military surgeon who supplied showmen in Britain with African animals. What made Sarah Baartman's body so unique that she was marketed as "the missing link between man and beast"?[32] Her buttocks. British and French audience members not only paid to gawk at her body but also physically poked and prodded her to discern whether her buttocks was, in fact, real.[33] Baartman's death in 1815 would not end the degrading treatment of her body. French anatomist Georges Cuvier dissected her body, not to discern the cause of her early death at twenty-five but to "prove the scientific supremacy of white men." Her preserved skeleton and a cast of her body were then displayed—buttocks facing the audience—in French museums until the 1970s.[34]

Baartman's Black body served as a symbol to whites that Black women are physically *other*. Such otherness distances Black women even further from whiteness, validating their positions at the bottom of a racial hierarchy within which whiteness reigns. Today, similar messages communicate the view of Black women's bodies as exotic, nonhuman "freaks of nature."[35] Consider Kala's account. Kala is a multiracial, queer Guyanese woman in her late twenties who married her high school sweetheart, a white man. Having dated in the mid-2000s, the AOL Instant

Messaging app played a key role in peer communication before the popularity of smartphones. She recalls repeated incidents in which her now-husband's friends exotified her body: "I remember being on the computer reading his, whatever they're called, the [AOL instant] messages before AIM went away. And I would be like, 'What is he saying about me?' And I would read messages like, 'Yo, what does it look like, like when you F her? Like, your white penis in her?' And I was like . . . [silence], but I couldn't say anything because I had been snooping."

These comments reinforce the notion that Kala's Black body is exotic compared to white women. More than mere "locker room talk" between teenage boys, the question here is clearly racialized. In theorizing everyday racism, Essed argues that it is experienced both directly and vicariously.[36] Although not directly said to Kala, the impact of finding the message stuck with her as if she had experienced it firsthand; she felt the internal jab of realizing her body was objectified because of her Blackness. In contrast to direct microaggressions, the perceived in-group safety and comfort that white men or women feel when speaking with other white people cannot be discounted. Because these behaviors and comments still convey negative gendered racialized slights, still reinforce the domination of whiteness, and are still, indirectly, experienced by the target, they fall within the definition of everyday racism, even if they are proximate at the time.

Such proximate microaggressions perpetrated by white men were especially common among respondents who had white spouses. Jasmine is a Caribbean Canadian physical therapist in her late thirties, married to a white Czech man. She shared that her husband, Jacob, once admitted that his white friend assumed her body was different than white women's. "He's a really nice guy, but he's like, really ignorant. He asked Jacob if it was different kissing a brown girl, and my husband. . . . I was like—it's so stupid—I was like, 'Did he really say that?'"

Again, we see evidence of a genuine belief that Black women's bodies are exotic. Unlike Asian women, their bodies are not seen as *foreign* per se but still othered, with white women remaining the standard by which both are measured. At the core of such assumptions is three centuries of harmful race science. Although humans are more genetically alike than different, race science has sought to justify social inequalities on the basis of alleged biological factors. If inequality is the result of biological differences, there's nothing we can do to change it and no guilt to be felt for its perpetuity. Historically, othering Black bodies (whether genitals, skull size, buttocks, or otherwise) has been used to justify social oppressions such as enslavement, involuntary sterilization, eugenics, and segregation.[37] However, race science is not just a pseudoscientific faux pas of the past; the implications of that very research are still circulating today.[38] When we understand the historical context of othering Black women's bodies, it becomes quite evident that even proximate microaggressions are not without lasting significance.

Conclusion

Like white women counterparts, white men engaged in microaggressive comments and behaviors toward Black and Asian women that demonstrates their adoption of white racial framing and the domination of white patriarchy. White men sexualized, exoticized, and tokenized Black and Asian women, viewing my respondents as mysterious sexual experiences to satisfy a racist curiosity. As demonstrated in their stories, queerness, motherhood, and even marriage to other white men did not protect them from microaggressions that solidified their status as gendered, racialized Other. Such exotification is rooted in the perseverance of controlling images that originally developed as justifications for imperialism, colonialism, and enslavement: all acts of racist terrorism that used violence, power, and the rape of women of color to further globalize white supremacist patriarchy.

Some may argue that such institutions are no longer at the forefront of race relations today, yet the same controlling images continue to shape the experiences of women of color who find themselves in the company of white men. We are a society that builds on itself; our relationships today are the product of our history. The media we consume, the conversations we have with friends, coworkers, and strangers, and who we find attractive and worthy are all dictated by the institutions from which our society was built—a society that has, from inception, validated and sustained a white racial hierarchy.[39]

Through the past three chapters, I have identified the unique ways in which white perpetrators microaggress Black and Asian women: white families both tokenize and dismiss nonwhite women's racialized experiences, white women perform Oppression Olympics, white saviorism, and a rigid subscription to controlling images, and white men see women of color as sexualized experiences rather than as complex, individual human beings. Each of these themes reflect the dominance of white racial framing where women of color are inferior, sexual objects, threatening, or unreasonable, ultimately painting women of color as uncivilized in contrast to white women's civility. These themes emerged regardless of whether the respondent was Black or Asian, queer or straight, and acquainted or unknown to the perpetrators.

I opened this chapter with a description of Robert Aaron Long's actions on March 16, 2021. I remember exactly what I was doing when news of the shootings broke. In the last semester of my graduate studies, I was working on the analysis for this book's research on my university's downtown Atlanta campus, only six miles away from Gold Spa. His decisions that day will likely not be studied by microaggression researchers; they were not subtle, they were not innocuous, and they were not backhanded compliments. But they were rooted in an ideology that centralizes the desires of white men and entitles them to space, time, bodies, and lives of women of color, and the macro social force that sustains that ideology is the very same that allows all women of color to continue to be at risk for violence, covert and not, at the hands of white men.

CHAPTER 10

"It's Ontological"

Moving Forward in Understanding Microaggressions

In the summer of 2020, after the murder of George Floyd and the wide societal unrest that followed, sales of Robin DiAngelo's *White Fragility* and other anti-racism books skyrocketed as anti-racist book clubs formed,[1] symbolic black squares were posted on Instagram feeds, and employers of all kinds posted job ads for diversity, equity, and inclusion (DEI) specialists—salaried positions to teach company employees about systemic racism, discriminatory hiring practices, and workplace microaggressions. I remember the influx of these positions quite clearly as a graduate student beginning my own journey on the job market.

Five years later, not only are those jobs are no longer in demand, but the inclusion of DEI programs across the country are under legal threat, and countless companies that rallied to promote their DEI advances in 2020 have scaled back or eliminated such programs entirely by 2025.[2] As much as I would like to live in a world where racism is solved one office DEI training at a time, studying racism and white supremacy has taught me to be much more pessimistic or, arguably, more realistic. These positions are not subsiding solely because the goals of anti-racism were met by each employee. Neither are they subsiding exclusively due to Donald Trump's opposition to them, as these roles were on the decline before his second presidential term began.[3] They are not decreasing because we have all learned to be less racist and aware of white privileges and thus there is less need for them. They are becoming less relevant because racism is adapting, and combating racism at an exclusively micro level is not going to solve the supremacy of whiteness.

Racial Realism

In this book, I have demonstrated critical race theorist Derrick Bell's concept of *racial realism* and the permanence of racism.[4] Racism does not dissipate but instead adapts to persevere. It is both, at once, invisible and highly visible. It operates through meso and micro systems to remain undefeated. Perhaps it is no longer socially acceptable to use racial slurs, but touching Black women's hair without an invitation is masked as a compliment. Formal segregation may no longer be legally dictated, but seeking out only Asian women as romantic partners is viewed as simply a matter of taste. On the surface, it is difficult to argue that the intent of the enactor is rooted in racism. And yet, as we pride ourselves on moving beyond Racism-with-a-capital-R, we ignore the not-so-unfamiliar metamorphosis: an ideology that Black and Asian women are *other*.

Based on the ordinary nature of racism, we can assume that microaggressions and other everyday racism will eventually evolve into something else as well; our microaggression trainings and DEI workshops guaranteed that. In early 2025, the political backlash against DEI programming simply reminds us that these trainings never challenged the foundation of white supremacy at all. Rather, they allowed us to check a box that afforded the comfort of feeling like we were doing *something*, without challenging the existing structure. Until racism is addressed at the systemic level, microinterventions to solve it arguably contribute to its perpetual reign.

The Boundaries of White Supremacy

The accounts my respondents shared demonstrate the boundaryless nature of white supremacy. The white racial frame is so prevalent that its ideology permeates even nonwhite spaces. In intraracial spaces, Black and Asian women face incessant microinteractions that reflect a pressure to conform to, assimilate to, or be adjacent to whiteness, from the food we eat, the names we go by, and the partners we choose to spend our lives with. Black and Asian American women are further expected to fit into stereotypical and typecast models of the "right" and "wrong" kind of Black or Asian—an expectation imposed on them by their own family and community members—to push their bodies into unnatural and impossible molds to fit those characteristics, shaped, defined, and assigned value by whiteness. On the other hand, in white spaces, Black and Asian women are exposed to microaggressions that reinforce color-blind narratives, fortify white saviorist ideologies of the unfortunate person of color in need of white charity, and sexualize tokenism and exotification. My respondents pointed to white women specifically as the most expected enactors of microaggressions, as well as the incidents that caused the most distress.

No space, relationship, or community is immune to perpetuating these messages. And each of these messages—though they may vary depending on the enactor and they may vary depending on the target—ultimately strengthens the domination of whiteness. The existence of "safe space" for women of color in the United States is, perhaps, wishful thinking. This matters. What respite do we have when there is no safe space from death by a thousand cuts?

Reconsidering the Obligation of Resilience and Resistance

Scholarship of racism often focuses on resistance and resilience strategies for targets, and microaggression research is no exception.[5] In my prior research examining microaggressions, I outlined the different strategies that my respondents used to build resilience and resistance from incessant microaggressions. Even Pierce himself argued that Black people facing routine mechanisms of racism should focus on constructing different futures that do not cater to internalized white supremacy.[6] But it is important to consider what these suggestions ask and of whom. Clearly, Black and Asian American women navigate responses to everyday racism on a regular basis; the "everyday" of *everyday racism* is not an exaggeration. Research confirms that exposure to such incessant discrimination is psychologically and physiologically taxing.[7] The cumulative nature of microaggressions ensures that victims' responses to them are not one and done but that each event recalls structural racial and gender inequities from which we seemingly cannot escape. A to-do list of resistance strategies only further asks women of color to live with or solve their own oppression.

It makes sense why we focus on resilience and resistance. Without them, we succumb to our positions of subordination; we accept our bound wrists, we do not strive for better conditions, we do not build better futures for ourselves and our loved ones. As Audre Lorde reminds us, the master's tools will never dismantle the master's house; resilience and resistance allow us to create our own tools.[8] Change happens through resistance efforts. We manage to survive the day through building resilience. As long as there has been oppression, there has been resilience and resistance.

But developing a thick skin is not solving the problem of white supremacy. Having to seek out joy to combat the psychological violence of racism puts parameters around our right to joy for the sake of joy. Feminist philosopher Susan

Bordo writes, "The postmodern inclination to emphasize and celebrate 'resistance' mystifies and normalizes domination."[9] Yes, we can celebrate resistance strategies, celebrate the areas within which we find joy, celebrate our ability to form coalitions when they have been cast as threats against us. Yet, the necessity of resistance speaks to the unyielding strength of white supremacy, and the obligation on targets of everyday racism to exercise strength further removes accountability and responsibility from the very people upholding white patriarchal domination.

Moving Forward

In their call to reconsider the role of microaggression research, sociologists Johnny Williams and David Embrick argue that racial microaggressions as a concept is itself anti-Black.[10] Noting the long history of Chester Pierce's erasure, as well as the almost exclusive focus on interpersonal interactions in modern microaggression discourse, they claim, "Racial microaggression discourse is a pseudonym for Black suffering that disappears the structures of white supremacy driving anti-Black violence."[11] Throughout this book, I have discussed examples of both specific incidents as well as comments and feelings that demonstrate my respondents' experiences with everyday racism, but these events and feelings recall a historical, hegemonic, and persistent domination of whiteness, which is more than the sum of its micro interaction parts. We cannot rely on individual responses, individual resilience tactics, individual resistance strategies, to combat such a social force. We cannot study the trees without acknowledging the conditions of the forest from which it was nurtured to grow. Instead, we must treat microaggressions as a public health issue as Pierce suggested we do.[12]

Critical race feminism, by way of critical race theory, posits that racism and sexism are ordinary and that dominant frameworks, thought, and ideologies (e.g., a white racial frame) determine social outcomes, often without conscious intention.[13] Thus, redressing microaggressions as micro, interpersonal phenomena is a moot point without considering the structural components that allow gendered racism to flourish. White supremacy, along with other macro forces such as cisheterosexism and patriarchy, are interlocking systemic forces that rely on and buttress one another to adapt, evolve, and prosper. Through gendered racist microaggressions, these foundational components of U.S. society defy resistance, surreptitiously thriving by gaslighting women of color.

Employing a critical race feminism perspective in this project illuminates the narratives and counterstories of Asian American and Black women's experiences with covert gendered racism. This emphasis on standpoint epistemologies ensured that the narratives of women of color (whose realities are often discounted or omitted entirely from research on Black or Asian American experiences and research on women's experiences) were validated and constructed as truth. This is especially important in microaggression research, as the covert nature of everyday racism allows perpetrators to deny that their comment or behavior was offensive.[14] This leaves Black and Asian American women, who have lived lifetimes of everyday racism to inform their understanding of its nuance, questioning their own realities, and such uncertainty further affirms white domination over women of color.

Evident in this journey is that micro interactions such as microaggressions operate as everyday racism to invisibilize, maintain, and prolong the macro social structure of white patriarchal supremacy, regardless of the spaces that Black and Asian American women occupy. We can surround ourselves with only intraracial friends and peers, avoid Racists-with-a-capital-R, drive out of our ways to see co-ethnic medical doctors and therapists, or live in parts of town with only neighbors who look like us, if such parts of town exist, yet none of these efforts will protect us from the incessant domineering force of white supremacy.

Philomena Essed writes, "In order to expose racism in the system it does not make sense to fight people, to wonder whether he or she is a racist. It is relevant to focus on when, where, and how racism operates through everyday life, how and when ordinary situations become racist situations. What I am claiming is that there is no structural racism without everyday racism."[15] Elucidated throughout my respondents' stories is the dominating nature of macro social forces: What makes microaggressions harmful is the way they recall the centuries-long domination of Black and Asian women by white supremacy. There is not one without the other; to focus solely on the micro is to ignore what makes it important to study at all.

ACKNOWLEDGMENTS

Though only one name sits on the cover, this book is a product of community.

Thank you mom and John, who both shower me with unyielding support in whatever form my dreams take. I could not have--would not have--pursued the graduate program from which this project began without your belief in me.

Thank you Tyler, who read every draft, offered alternatives for every funny use of an ill-fitting word, fed and nurtured me, and brought me to hikes and sunshine through the years of collecting and putting together these stories. Thank you for loving me. Thank you to my pets--Tokie, Banksy, Penny, Pogo, and Yarra—and my fosters—Autumn, Callie, Bertie, Albert, and Saundi—for being warm and fuzzy things I could bury my face into at the end of the day.

I am honored to be surrounded by a community of friends who have, at some point or another, also been mentors to me. Thank you, alithia zamantakis, Monisha Jackson, Kara Tsukerman, Tabitha Ingle, and Ebony Respress, for talking through tough theory with me, for sending groceries and takeout and flowers to my house when I was knee-deep in analysis and forgetting to nourish my body, for drinking yard-garitas with me to get through dissertating during a pandemic, and for singing all-night karaoke with me in Koreatown. Thank you for challenging me to be a better scholar, teacher, activist, and friend. Thank you also to Sophia Krieg, Sarah Gelder, and Stephanie LaFave, who have loved every iteration of me for the past twenty-plus years without question. Thank you all for being my family.

Thank you, Rosalind Chou, Katie Acosta, and Veronica Newton, who guided the early inceptions of this project and encouraged me to be unapologetic in what the data revealed. Thank you, Cameron Lippard, who I am lucky to call a mentor, colleague, and friend. You have funneled so many open doors to me, and it is you I credit (blame, perhaps) for growing my love for sociology and bringing me back to this field. Thank you, Marisela Martinez-Cola. I was a stranger to you when I signed the contract for this book, and you welcomed me so warmly into your circle. I am so appreciative of your guidance and honored to share a space in this series beside you; without you, this book would not have its name.

Thank you, Jasmine Gibbs, my research assistant who transcribed many of these interviews without complaint. I am so proud of the scholar and person you have become. When I see your success and happiness, it makes my heart BEAM!

It is such an immense privilege to be a part of the Race and Ethnicity Series at the University of Georgia Press. Early on in my graduate program, "The Davids" came to my department to discuss this book series. I pitched two potential projects to them, with one in mind that I was more confident to pursue. David Brunsma repeatedly circled back to the project I had all but decided to abandon. That is this project. Thank you, David, for seeing where this could go and all your mentorship since then. Thank you to Mick Duffy, to my early reviewers, and to the Series Advisory Board: Margaret Abraham, Elijah Anderson, Eduardo Bonilla-Silva, Philomena Essed, James Fenelon, Tanya Golash-Boza, David Theo Goldberg, Patricia Hill Collins, Jose Itzigsohn, Amanda Lewis, Michael Omi, Victor Rios, and Mary Romero. Your own work is an inspiration to me, and because of you, this book feels right at home with UGA Press.

I was only able to write this book because of the stories granted to me by my thirty-five respondents. Thank you, for allowing me into your communities, for reliving your experiences with me, for laughing and sighing and being vulnerable with me. Through many of our conversations, my own experiences were also seen. Thank you, for trusting me to write these stories.

NOTES

Chapter 1. "You're One of *Those*": Microaggressions and Macroimplications

1. Derrick Bell (1992), *Faces at the Bottom of the Well: The Permanence of Racism* (New York, N.Y.: Basic Books).

2. Joe Feagin and Melvin P. Sikes (1994), *Living with Racism: The Black Middle-Class Experience* (Boston, Mass.: Beacon Press). See also Joe R. Feagin (2009), *Systemic Racism: A Theory of Oppression* (New York, N.Y.: Routledge); Augie Fleras (2016), "Theorizing Micro-Aggressions as Racism 3.0: Shifting the Discourse," *Canadian Ethnic Studies, 48*(2): 1–19.

3. Eduardo Bonilla-Silva (2014), *Racism Without Racists: Color-Blind Racism and the Persistence of Racial Inequality in America* (Lanham, Md.: Rowman & Littlefield). I have chosen to capitalize "Black" and not "white" throughout this document to give authority to a marginalized group and to indicate an identity that is not ubiquitous with whites. See footnote 6 on p. 1244 of *Mapping the Margins: Intersectionality, Identity Politics, and Violence Against Women of Color* by Kimberlé Crenshaw for more info.

4. Derald W. Sue, Christina M. Capodilupo, Gina C. Torino, Jennifer M. Bucceri, Aisha M. B. Holder, Kevin L. Nadal, and Marta Equilin (2007), "Racial Microaggressions in Everyday Life: Implications for Clinical Practice," *American Psychologist 62*(4): 271–286.

5. Johnny E. Williams and David G. Embrick (2023), "Moving Beyond Obfuscating Racial Microaggression Discourse," *Social Inclusion, 11*(2): 5–15.

6. Chester M. Pierce (1970), "Offensive Mechanisms," in *The Black Seventies*, ed. Floyd B. Barbour (Boston, Mass.: Porter Sargent), 276.

7. Philomena Essed (1991), *Understanding Everyday Racism: An Interdisciplinary Theory* (Newbury Park, Calif.: Sage).

8. Ibid.

9. Ibid, 207.

10. Philomena Essed (2008), "Everyday Racism," in *A Companion to Racial and Ethnic Studies*, ed. D. T. Goldberg and J. Solomos, 202–216 (Malden, Mass.: Blackwell).

11. Essed, *Understanding Everyday Racism*; Pierce 1970: 265–282; Silvia Domínguez and David G. Embrick (2020), "Racial Microaggressions: Bridging Psychology and Sociology and Future Research Considerations," *Sociology Compass*, *14*(8): 1–14.

12. Pierce, "Offensive Mechanisms," 265–282; Chester M. Pierce (1974), "Psychiatric Problems of the Black Minority," in *American Handbook of Psychiatry*, ed. S. Arieti, 512–523 (New York, N.Y.: Basic Books); Essed, *Understanding Everyday Racism*; Philomena Essed (1990), *Everyday Racism: Reports from Women of Two Cultures* (Alameda, Calif.: Hunter House).

13. Johnny E. Williams (2015), "Talking About Race Without Talking About Race: Color Blindness in Genomics," *American Behavioral Scientist*, *59*(11): 1496–1517.

14. Claire Jean Kim, *Asian Americans in an Anti-Black World* (New York, N.Y.: Cambridge University Press, 2023), 10; emphasis original.

15. Pierce, "Offensive Mechanisms," 265–282.

16. Domínguez and Embrick, "Racial Microaggressions," 1–14.

17. Williams and Embrick, "Moving Beyond Obfuscating Racial Microaggression Discourse," 5–15.

18. David Embrick, Silvia Domínguez, and Baran Karsak (2017), "More than Just Insult: Rethinking Sociology's Contribution to Scholarship on Racial Microaggressions," *Sociological Inquiry*, *87*(2): 193–206.

19. Ron Taffel (2020), "The Myth of Micro-Aggression," *Contemporary Psychoanalysis*, *56*(2–3): 375–393.

20. Pierce, "Offensive Mechanisms," 276; Pierce, "Psychiatric Problems of the Black Minority," 520.

21. Essed, *Understanding Everyday Racism*; See also Daniel G. Solórzano and Lindsay Pérez Huber (2020), *Racial Microaggressions: Using Critical Race Theory to Respond to Everyday Racism* (New York, N.Y.: Teachers College Press) and Williams and Embrick, "Moving Beyond Obfuscating Racial Microaggression Discourse," 5–15.

22. The nickname "Karen" refers to (mostly) white women who call police on, or otherwise harass, people of color and primarily Black people existing normally in predominantly white spaces. See Jessie Daniels (2021), *Nice White Ladies: The Truth About White Supremacy, Our Role in It, and How We Can Help Dismantle It* (New York, N.Y.: Seal Press).

23. Shannon Sullivan (2014), *Good White People: The Problem with Middle-Class White Anti-Racism* (New York, N.Y.: State University of New York Press), 4.

24. Pierce, "Offensive Mechanisms," 276.

25. Chester M. Pierce (1995), "Stress Analogs of Racism and Sexism: Terrorism, Torture, and Disaster," in *Mental Health, Racism, and Sexism*, ed. Charles V. White, Patricia Perri Rieker, Bernard M. Karmer, and Bertram S. Brown, (Pittsburgh, Pa.: University of Pittsburgh Press), 277.

26. Embrick, Domínguez, and Karsak, "More than Just Insult," 193–206.

27. Ibid., 194.

28. Domínguez and Embrick, "Racial Microaggressions," 2.

29. This concept is an anti-Black response to the civil rights era in which Asian immigrants were deemed "good" people of color in contrast to Black Americans being cast as "bad" people of color. See also *The Myth of the Model Minority* by Rosalind Chou and Joe Feagin and *Asian Americans in an Anti-Black World* by Claire Jean Kim for more.

30. Victoria Reyes (2022), *Academic Outsider: Stories of Exclusion and Hope* (Stanford, Calif.: Stanford University Press), 7.

31. Feagin, *Systemic Racism*; Pierce, "Offensive Mechanisms," 265–282; Essed, *Understanding Everyday Racism*; Sue et al., "Racial Microaggressions in Everyday Life," 271–286.

32. Joe R. Feagin (2013), *The White Racial Frame: Centuries of Racial Framing and Counter-Framing* (New York, N.Y.: Routledge).

Chapter 2. Theoretical Perspectives on Microaggressions and Everyday Racism

1. Chester M. Pierce (1970), "Offensive Mechanisms," in *The Black Seventies*, ed. Floyd B. Barbour, 265–282 (Boston, Mass.: Porter Sargent). See also Derald W. Sue (2010), *Microaggressions in Everyday Life: Race, Gender, and Sexual Orientation* (Hoboken, N.J.: Wiley) and Derald W. Sue (2010), *Microaggressions and Marginality* (Hoboken, N.J.: Wiley).

2. bell hooks (1994), *Teaching to Transgress: Education as the Practice of Freedom* (New York, N.Y.: Routledge), 59.

3. Charles W. Mills (1997), *The Racial Contract* (New York, N.Y.: Cornell University Press).

4. Joe. R. Feagin (2013), *The White Racial Frame: Centuries of Racial Framing and Counter-Framing* (New York, N.Y.: Routledge).

5. Kwame Ture and Charles V. Hamilton (1992), *Black Power: The Politics of Liberation* (New York, N.Y.: Vintage).

6. Joe R. Feagin (2009), *Systemic Racism: A Theory of Oppression* (New York, N.Y.: Routledge).

7. Ibid.

8. Feagin, *The White Racial Frame*.

9. Ibid.

10. Ibid.

11. Ibid.

12. Eduardo Bonilla-Silva (2022), *Racism Without Racists: Color-Blind Racism and the Persistence of Racial Inequality in America* (Lanham, Md.: Rowman & Littlefield).

13. Patricia Hill Collins (2000), *Black Feminist Thought: Knowledge, Consciousness and the Politics of Empowerment* (New York, N.Y.: Routledge).

14. Patricia Hill Collins (1986), "Learning from the Outsider Within: The Sociological Significance of Black Feminist Thought," *Social Problems, 33*(6): S14–S32.

15. Collins, *Black Feminist Thought*, 69.

16. Ibid.

17. Dresden Lackey and Rosalind Chou (2019), "Foreign, Fetishized, Fever! An Examination of the Exotification of Asian and Asian American Women by White Men in the U.S.," in *The Yellow Book*, ed. Isaac Chong, 283–302 (Berlin: He Xiangyu Studio). See also Ruby Hamad (2020), *White Tears, Brown Scars: How White Feminism Harms Women of Color* (New York, N.Y.: Catapult).

18. Collins, *Black Feminist Thought*.

19. Patricia Hill Collins (1995), "Symposium: On West and Fenstermaker's Doing Difference," *Gender & Society, 9*(4): 492.

20. Patrick Grzanka (ed.) (2019), *Intersectionality: Foundations and Frontiers* (New York, N.Y.: Routledge). See also Anna Carastathis (2016), *Intersectionality: Origins, Contestations, Horizons* (Lincoln, Nebr.: University of Nebraska Press).

21. Richard Delgado and Jean Stafancic (2012), *Critical Race Theory: An Introduction* (New York, N.Y.: New York University Press).

22. Adrien Katherine Wing (ed.) (2003), *Critical Race Feminism: A Reader*, 2nd ed. (New York, N.Y.: New York University Press).

23. Philomena Essed (1991), *Understanding Everyday Racism: An Interdisciplinary Theory* (Newbury Park, Calif.; Sage).

24. Ibid.

25. Sue, *Microaggressions and Marginality*. See also Sue, *Microaggressions in Everyday Life*.

26. Collins, *Black Feminist Thought*; Essed, *Understanding Everyday Racism*.

27. Jioni A. Lewis, Ruby Mendenhall, Stacy A. Harwood, and Margaret Browne Huntt (2016), "'Ain't I a Woman?': Perceived Gendered Racial Microaggressions Experienced by Black Women," *The Counseling Psychologist, 44*(5): 758–780. Note: In my own writing, I refer to gendered racial microaggressions as gendered racist microaggressions to name "racism" as distinct from the general "racial."

28. Rosalind Chou (2012), *Asian American Sexual Politics* (Lanham, Md.: Rowman & Littlefield).

29. Collins, *Black Feminist Thought*. See also Sue, *Microaggressions and Marginality*.

30. Collins, *Black Feminist Thought*, 284.

31. Thomas R. Bates (1975), "Gramsci and the Theory of Hegemony," *Journal of the History of Ideas, 36*(2): 351–366. See also Chou, *Asian American Sexual Politics*.

32. Audre Lorde (1984), *Sister Outsider* (New York, N.Y.: Ten Speed Press).

33. Kimberlé W. Crenshaw, Andrea J. Ritchie, Rachel Anspach, Rachel Gilmer, and Luke Harris (2015), *Say Her Name: Resisting Police Brutality Against Black Women*. Report available at https://scholarship.law.columbia.edu/faculty_scholarship/3226.

Chapter 3. Moving Toward Whiteness

1. Elijah Anderson (2015), "The White Space," *Sociology of Race and Ethnicity, 1*(1): 10–21.

2. Joe R. Feagin (2013), *The White Racial Frame: Centuries of Racial Framing and Counter-Framing* (New York, N.Y.: Routledge).

3. Chester M. Pierce (1970), "Offensive Mechanisms," in *The Black Seventies*, ed. Floyd B. Barbour, 265–282 (Boston, Mass.: Porter Sargent); Philomena Essed (1991), *Understanding Everyday Racism: An Interdisciplinary Theory* (Newbury Park, Calif.; Sage).

4. Derald W. Sue (2010), *Microaggressions in Everyday Life: Race, Gender, and Sexual Orientation* (Hoboken, N.J.: Wiley).

5. Joe R. Feagin (2009), *Systemic Racism: A Theory of Oppression* (New York, N.Y.: Routledge).

6. Pierce, "Offensive Mechanisms," 265–282.

7. Ibid., 277.

8. Ibid.

9. Sue, *Microaggressions in Everyday Life*.

10. https://www.scoopwhoop.com/humor/white-people-dont-wash-legs-twitter-reactions/

11. Rosalind Chou and Joe R. Feagin (2008), *The Myth of the Model Minority: Asian Americans Facing Racism* (Boulder, Colo.: Paradigm).

12. Rosalind Chou (2012), *Asian American Sexual Politics* (Lanham, Md.: Rowman & Littlefield).

13. R. W. Connell (2005), *Masculinities*, 2nd ed. (Berkeley: University of California Press).

14. Matthew W. Hughey (2011), "Backstage Discourse and the Reproduction of White Masculinities," *Sociological Quarterly*, *52*: 134.

15. Chou, *Asian American Sexual Politics*.

16. Ibid.

17. Adrienne Rich (1980), "Compulsory Heterosexuality and the Lesbian Existence," *Journal of Women's History*, *15*(3): 11–48.

18. Chou, *Asian American Sexual Politics*.

19. Jerry A. Jacobs and Teresa G Labov (2002), "Gender Differentials in Intermarriage Among Sixteen Race and Ethnic Groups," *Sociological Forum*, *17*: 621–646.

20. Chou, *Asian American Sexual Politics*.

21. See Claire Jean Kim (2000), *Bitter Fruit: The Politics of Black-Korean Conflict in New York City* (New Haven, Conn.: Yale University Press).

22. Chou, *Asian American Sexual Politics*. See also Patricia Hill Collins (2000), *Black Feminist Thought: Knowledge, Consciousness and the Politics of Empowerment* (New York, N.Y.: Routledge).

23. Collins, *Black Feminist Thought*.

24. Gretchen Livingston and Anna Brown (May 18, 2017), "Intermarriage in the U.S. 50 Years After *Loving v. Virginia*," Pew Research Center, https://www.pewresearch.org/social-trends/2017/05/18/1-trends-and-patterns-in-intermarriage/. Note that Black husband–white wife couples are over twice as common at 7 percent of all interracially married couples.

25. Chester M. Pierce (1974), "Psychiatric Problems of the Black Minority," in *American Handbook of Psychiatry*, ed. S. Arieti (New York, N.Y.: Basic Books), 7.

26. Ruth Frankenberg (2001), "The Mirage of an Unmarked Whiteness," in *The Making and Unmaking of Whiteness*, ed. Birgit Brander Rasmussen, Eric Klinenberg, Irene J Nexica, and Matt Wray, 73–96 (Durham, N.C.: Duke University Press).

27. Pierce, "Offensive Mechanisms."

28. Richard Dyer (2017), *White* (New York, N.Y.: Routledge).

29. Sue, *Microaggressions in Everyday Life*.

30. https://www.imdb.com/title/tt10856734/

31. J. Camille Hall and Jandel Crutchfield (2018), "Black Women's Experience of Colorist Microaggressions," *Social Work in Mental Health*, *16*(4): 491–503.

32. Ibid.

33. Chou and Feagin, *The Myth of the Model Minority*.

34. Frantz Fanon (2008), *Black Skin, White Masks* (New York, N.Y.: Grove).

35. Tayler J. Matthews and Glenn Johnson (2015), "Skin Complexion in the Twenty First Century: The Impact of Colorism on African American Women," *Race, Gender, & Class*, *22*(1–2): 248–274. See also Mark E. Hill (2002), "Skin Color and the Perception of Attractiveness Among African Americans: Does Gender Make a Difference?" *Social Psychology Quarterly*, *65*(1): 77–91.

36. Hill, "Skin Color and the Perception of Attractiveness."

37. Hall and Crutchfield, "Black Women's Experience of Colorist Microaggressions."

38. Margaret Hunter (2007), "The Persistent Problem of Colorism: Skin Tone, Status, and Inequality," *Sociology Compass, 1*(1): 237–254. See also Jennifer L. Hochschild and Velsa Weaver (2007), "The Skin Color Paradox and the American Racial Order," *Social Forces, 86*(2): 643–670.

39. Collins, *Black Feminist Thought.*

40. Imani Tafari-Ama (2016), "Historical Sociology of Beauty Practices: Internalized Racism, Skin Bleaching, and Hair Straightening," *IDEAZ, 14*: 1–19.

41. Chou, *Asian American Sexual Politics.*

42. George Lipsitz (2018), *The Possessive Investment in Whiteness: How White People Profit from Identity Politics* (Philadelphia, Pa.: Temple University Press), 2.

Chapter 4. The Right and Wrong Kind

1. W. E. B. Du Bois (2014), *The Problem of the Color Line at the Turn of the Twentieth Century: The Essential Early Essays*, edited by Nahum Dimitri Chandler (New York, N.Y.: Fordham University Press). See also Wolfgage Umek and Barbara Fischer (2020), "We Should Abandon 'Race' as a Biological Category in Biomedical Research," *Female Pelvic Medicine and Reconstructive Surgery, 26*(12): 719–720.

2. Ian Haney Lopez (2006), *White by Law: The Legal Construction of Race* (New York, N.Y.: New York University Press).

3. *Takao Ozawa v. United States*, 260 U.S. 178 (1922).

4. *United States v. Thind*, 261 U.S. 204 (1923).

5. *Racial Integrity Act of 1924*, State Legislature of Virginia.

6. Pauli Murray (ed.) (2016), *States' Laws on Race and Color* (Athens: University of Georgia Press).

7. Marc P. Johnston and Kevin Nadal (2010), "Multiracial Microaggressions: Exposing Monoracism in Everyday Life and Clinical Practice," in *Microaggressions and Marginality*, ed. Derald W. Sue, 123–144 (Hoboken, N.J.: Wiley).

8. George Lipsitz (2018), *The Possessive Investment in Whiteness: How White People Profit from Identity Politics* (Philadelphia, Pa.: Temple University Press). See also Robin DiAngelo (2010), "Why Can't We All Just Be Individuals? Countering the Discourse of Individualism in Anti-Racist Education," *InterActions: UCLA Journal of Education and Information Studies, 6*(1).

9. Lucy Tse (2000), "The Effects of Ethnic Identity Formation on Bilingual Maintenance and Development: An Analysis of Asian American Narratives," *International Journal of Bilingual Education and Bilingualism, 3*(3): 185–200.

10. Eileen O'Brien (2008), *The Racial Middle: Latinos and Asian Americans Living Beyond the Racial Divide* (New York, N.Y.: New York University Press).

11. Karen Pyke and Tran Dang (2003), "'FOB' and 'Whitewashed': Identity and Internalized Racism Among Second Generation Asian Americans," *Qualitative Sociology, 26*(2): 147–172.

12. Ibid.

13. W. E. B. Du Bois (1994), *The Souls of Black Folk* (New York, N.Y.: Dover).

14. The Seoulmal dialect, also referred to as the Gyeonggi dialect, is primarily used in the Seoul capital of South Korea, although more recently it is being used across regions. Nari's classmates judge her use of a more southern, rural Korean dialect in their criticisms of her.

15. Suah Kim and Rachel H. Kim (2010), "Microaggressions Experienced by International Students Attending U.S. Institutions of Higher Education," in *Microaggressions and Marginality*, ed. Derald W. Sue, 171–191 (Hoboken, N.J.: Wiley); Derald W. Sue (2010), *Microaggressions in Everyday Life: Race, Gender, and Sexual Orientation* (Hoboken, N.J.: Wiley).

16. Shannon Sullivan (2006), *Revealing Whiteness: The Unconscious Habits of Racial Privilege* (Bloomington: Indiana University Press).

17. Shardé Davis (2019), "When Sistahs Support Sistahs: A Process of Supportive Communication About Racial Microaggressions Among Black Women," *Communication Monographs, 86*(2): 133–157.

18. Joe R. Feagin (2009), *Systemic Racism: A Theory of Oppression* (New York, N.Y.: Routledge).

19. Chester M. Pierce (1974), "Psychiatric Problems of the Black Minority," in *American Handbook of Psychiatry*, ed. by S. Arieti (New York, N.Y.: Basic Books), 7.

20. Rosalind Chou and Joe Feagin (2008), *The Myth of the Model Minority: Asian Americans Facing Racism* (Boulder, Colo.: Paradigm).

21. Ibid.

22. Patricia Hill Collins (2000), *Black Feminist Thought: Knowledge, Consciousness and the Politics of Empowerment* (New York, N.Y.: Routledge).

23. Pierce, "Psychiatric Problems of the Black Minority," 10–11.

24. Derald W. Sue (ed.) (2010), *Microaggressions and Marginality* (Hoboken, N.J.: Wiley).

25. Sullivan, *Revealing Whiteness*, 10.

26. Chris Cross-Zimmerman, Devon Thomas, Elizabeth A. Collins, and Nolan L. Cabrera (2020), "Ontological Expansiveness," in *Encyclopedia of Critical Whiteness Studies in Education*, vol. 2, ed. Zachary A. Casey, chap. 58 (Boston, Mass.: Brill).

27. Margaret Hunter (2007), "The Persistent Problem of Colorism: Skin Tone, Status, and Inequality," *Sociology Compass, 1*(1): 237–254.

28. DiAngelo (2010), "Why Can't We All Just Be Individuals? Countering the Discourse of Individualism in Anti-Racist Education," *InterActions: UCLA Journal of Education and Information Studies, 6*(1).

29. Richard Dyer (2017), *White* (New York, N.Y.: Routledge).

Chapter 5. Body Talk

1. Patricia Hill Collins (2000), *Black Feminist Thought: Knowledge, Consciousness and the Politics of Empowerment* (New York, N.Y.: Routledge).

2. Ibid. See also Karen D. Pyke and Denise L. Johnson (2003), "Asian American Women and Racialized Femininities: 'Doing' Gender Across Cultural Worlds," *Gender & Society, 17*(1): 33–53.

3. Karen D. Pyke and Denise L. Johnson (2003), "Asian American Women and Racialized Femininities: 'Doing' Gender Across Cultural Worlds," *Gender & Society, 17*(1): 33–53.

4. Mimi Schippers (2007), "Recovering the Feminine Other: Masculinity, Femininity, and Gender Hegemony," *Theory and Society, 36*(1): 85–102.

5. Rosalind Chou (2012), *Asian American Sexual Politics* (Lanham, Md.: Rowman & Littlefield).

6. Schippers, "Recovering the Feminine Other." See also Ruth Frankenberg (1993), *White Women, Race Matters* (Minneapolis: University of Minnesota Press).

7. Hope Landrine (1985), "Race x Class Stereotypes of Women," *Sex Roles: A Journal of Research, 13*(1–2): 65–75. See also Collins, *Black Feminist Thought* and Schippers, "Recovering the Feminine Other."

8. bell hooks (2003), *We Real Cool: Black Men and Masculinity* (New York, N.Y.: Routledge).

9. David L. Eng (2001), *Racial Castration: Managing Masculinity in Asian America* (Durham, N.C.: Duke University Press).

10. Patricia Hill Collins (2004), *Black Sexual Politics: African Americans, Gender, and the New Racism* (New York, N.Y.: Routledge).

11. Annecka Marshall (1995), "From Sexual Denigration to Self-Respect: Resisting Images of Black Female Sexuality," in *Reconstructing Womanhood, Reconstructing Feminism: Writings on Black Women*, ed. Delia Jarrett-Macauley (New York, N.Y.: Routledge), 5.

12. Collins, *Black Sexual Politics*.

13. Joe R. Feagin (2000), *Racist America: Roots, Current Realities, and Future Reparations* (New York, N.Y.: Routledge). See also Collins, *Black Sexual Politics*.

14. Sabrina Strings (2019), *Killing the Black Body* (New York, N.Y.: New York University Press).

15. Ibid., 6.

16. Ibid. See also Aubrey Gordon (2020), *What We Don't Talk About When We Talk About Fat* (Boston, Mass.: Beacon).

17. Chelsie E. Dunn, Kristina B. Hood, and Bianca D. Owens (2018), "Loving Myself Through Thick and Thin: Appearance Contingent Self-Worth, Gendered Racial Microaggressions and African American Women's Body Appreciation," *Body Image, 30*: 121–126.

18. Strings, *Killing the Black Body*.

19. Margo Okazawa-Rey, Tracy Robinson, and Janie Victoria Ward (1987), "Black Women and the Politics of Skin Color and Hair," *Women and Therapy, 6*: 89–102. See also Althea Prince (2010), *The Politics of Black Women's Hair* (London, ON: Insomniac Press).

20. Nell Painter (2010), *The History of White People* (New York, N.Y.: Norton).

21. Rhonda Baynes Jeffries and Devair Jeffries (2014), "Reclaiming Our Roots: The Influences of Media Curriculum on the Natural Hair Movement," *Multicultural Perspectives, 16*(3): 160–165.

22. Kassidie Harmon (2020), "The Effect of Natural Hair on Stereotype Activation" (bachelor's thesis, Ohio State University).

23. Jared Council (November 4, 2022), "Black Women Going Natural Push Entire Industry to the Brink of Extinction," *Forbes*, https://www.forbes.com/sites/jaredcouncil/2022/11/04/black-women-going-natural-push-entire-industry-to-the-brink-of-extinction/?sh=1ee8fc101434.

24. Che-Jung Chang, Katie M. O'Brien, Alexander P. Keil, Symielle A. Gatson, Chandra L. Jackson, Dale P. Sandler, and Alexandra J. White (2022), "Use of Hair Straighteners and Other Hair Products and Incident Uterine Cancer," *Journal of the National Cancer Institute, 114*(12): 1636–1645.

25. Evelyn Brooks Higginbotham (1993), *Righteous Discontent: The Women's Movement in the Black Baptist Church, 1880–1920* (Cambridge, Mass.: Harvard University Press).

26. Barbara Harris Combs (2022), *Bodies Out of Place* (Athens: University of Georgia Press).

27. Christy Zhou Koval and Ashleigh Shelby Rosette (2020), "The Natural Hair Bias in Job Recruitment" *Social Psychology and Personality Science, 12*(5): 741–750.

28. Joane Nagel (2003), *Race, Ethnicity, and Sexuality: Intimate Intersections, Forbidden Frontiers* (New York, N.Y.: Oxford University Press).

29. Collins, *Black Sexual Politics.*

30. R. W. Connell (2005), *Masculinities*, 2nd ed. (Berkeley: University of California Press).

Chapter 6. The Role of Internalized Racism in Interracial Microaggressions

1. Joe R. Feagin (2013). *The White Racial Frame: Centuries of Racial Framing and Counter-Framing* (New York, N.Y.: Routledge).

2. Keith Osajima (1993), "The Hidden Injuries of Race," in *Bearing Dreams, Shaping Visions: Asian Pacific American Perspectives*, ed. L. Revilla, G. Nomura, S. Wong, and S. Hune, 81–91 (Pullman: Washington State University Press). See also bell hooks (2003), *Rock My Soul: Black People and Self-Esteem* (New York, N.Y.: Atria) and Karen D. Pyke (2010), "What Is Internalized Racial Oppression and Why Don't We Study It? Acknowledging Racism's Hidden Injuries," *Sociological Perspectives, 53*(4): 551–572.

3. Ruby Hamad (2020), *White Tears, Brown Scars: How White Feminism Harms Women of Color* (New York, N.Y.: Catapult), 206.

4. Chester M. Pierce (1995), "Stress Analogs of Racism and Sexism: Terrorism, Torture, and Disaster," in *Mental Health, Racism, and Sexism*, ed. Charles V. White, Patricia Perri Rieker, Bernard M. Karmer, and Bertram S. Brown, 277–293 (Pittsburgh, Pa.: University of Pittsburgh Press).

5. Franz Fanon (1961), *Wretched of the Earth* (New York, N.Y.: Grove).

6. Ruby Hamad (2020), *White Tears, Brown Scars: How White Feminism Harms Women of Color* (New York, N.Y.: Catapult).

7. Pyke, "What Is Internalized Racial Oppression."

8. E. J. R. David, Jessica Petalio, and Maria C. Crouch (2019), "Microaggressions and Internalized Oppression: Intrapersonal, Interpersonal, and Institutional Impacts of 'Internalized Microaggressions,'" in *Microaggression Theory: Influence and Implications*, ed. G. Torino, D. P. Rivera, C. M. Capodilupo, K. Nadal, and D. W. Sue, 121–137 (Hoboken, N.J.: Wiley).

9. Pierce, "Stress Analogs of Racism and Sexism."

10. E. J. R. David and Annie O. Derthick (2017), *The Psychology of Oppression* (New York, N.Y.: Springer).

11. David, Petalio, and Crouch, "Microaggressions and Internalized Oppression." See also Pyke, "What Is Internalized Racial Oppression."

12. David and Derthick, *The Psychology of Oppression.*

13. Pyke, "What Is Internalized Racial Oppression."

14. Daniel G. Solórzano and Lindsay Pérez Huber (2020), *Racial Microaggressions: Using Critical Race Theory to Respond to Everyday Racism* (New York, N.Y.: Teachers College Press), 105.

15. David, Petalio, and Crouch, "Microaggressions and Internalized Oppression," 130.

16. Chester M. Pierce (1974), "Psychiatric Problems of the Black Minority," in *American Handbook of Psychiatry*, ed. S. Arieti (New York, N.Y.: Basic Books), 7.

17. Feagin, *The White Racial Frame.*

Chapter 7. Compliments of the (White) House

1. Ruth Frankenberg (2001), "The Mirage of an Unmarked Whiteness," in *The Making and Unmaking of Whiteness*, ed. Birgit Brander Rasmussen, Eric Klinenberg, Irene J. Nexica, and Matt Wray, chap. 4 (Durham, N.C.: Duke University Press).

2. Elijah Anderson (2015), "The White Space," *Sociology of Race and Ethnicity*, *1*(1): 10–21.

3. David Brunsma, Nathaniel G. Chapman, Joong Won Kim, J. Slade Lellock, Megan Underhill, Erik T. Withers, and Jennifer Padilla Wyse (2020), "The Culture of White Space: On the Racialized Production of Meaning," *American Behavioral Scientist*, *64*(14): 2001–2015.

4. Ibid.

5. Barbara Harris Combs (2022), *Bodies Out of Place: Theorizing Anti-Blackness in U.S. Society* (Athens: University of Georgia Press).

6. Anderson, "The White Space."

7. Andrew D. Case and Carla D. Hunter (2012), "Counterspaces: A Unit of Analysis for Understanding the Role of Settings in Marginalized Individuals' Adaptive Responses to Oppression," *American Journal of Community Psychology*, *50*: 257–270; Patricia Hill Collins (2000), *Black Feminist Thought: Knowledge, Consciousness and the Politics of Empowerment* (New York, N.Y.: Routledge); bell hooks (1990), *Yearning: Race, Gender, and Cultural Politics* (New York, N.Y.: Routledge).

8. bell hooks, *Yearning*.

9. Eduardo Bonilla-Silva (2022), *Racism Without Racists: Colorblind Racism and the Persistence of Racial Inequality in America*, 6th ed. (Lanham, Md.: Rowman & Littlefield).

10. Shannon Sullivan (2014), *Good White People: The Problem with Middle-Class White Anti-Racism* (New York, N.Y.: State University of New York Press), 98.

11. Jiannbin Lee Shiao, Mia Tuan, and Elizabeth Rienzi (2004), "Shifting the Spotlight: Exploring Race and Culture in Korean-White Adoptive Families," *Race & Society*, 7: 1–16.

12. Pew Research Center, retrieved July 2023, https://www.pewresearch.org/interactives/what-census-calls-us/.

13. American Girl Fandom. Just like You #4 Doll, https://americangirl.fandom.com/wiki/Just_Like_You_4. This doll was subsequently retired in 2011. In 2007, American Girl debuted Ivy Ling, a Chinese American girl, on their historical line and thus accompanied with short books telling her story. Ivy was then discontinued in 2014.

14. Rosalind Chou and Joe Feagin (2008), *The Myth of the Model Minority: Asian Americans Facing Racism* (Boulder, Colo.: Paradigm).

15. Kenneth B. Clark and Mamie P. Clark (1950), "Emotional Factors in Racial Identification and Preference in Negro Children," *Journal of Negro Education*, *19*(3): 341.

16. Ibid.

17. SunAh M. Laybourn (2024), *Out of Place: The Lives of Korean Adoptee Immigrants* (New York, N.Y.: New York University Press), 8.

18. Sullivan, *Good White People*, 86.

19. Ibid., 91.

20. Shiao, Tuan, Rienzi, "Shifting the Spotlight."

21. Eduardo Bonilla-Silva (2004), "From Bi-Racial to Tri-Racial: Towards a New System of Stratification in the USA," *Ethnic and Racial Studies*, *27*(6): 931–950.

22. "The 60th Academy Awards (1988) Nominees and Winners," Academy of Motion Picture Arts and Sciences, https://www.oscars.org/oscars/ceremonies/1988.

23. Billboard.com Artist Chart History.

24. Bonilla- Silva, *Racism Without Racists.*

25. Coalition Building Among People of Color: A Discussion with Angela Y. Davis and Elizabeth Martínez (May 12, 1993), https://culturalstudies.ucsc.edu/inscriptions/volume-7/angela-y-davis-elizabeth-martinez/.

26. Anna Purna Kambhampaty (June 25, 2020), "'I Will Not Stand Silent.' 10 Asian Americans Reflect on Racism During the Pandemic and the Need for Equality," *Time*, https://time.com/5858649/racism-coronavirus.

27. Joe R. Feagin (2013), *The White Racial Frame: Centuries of Racial Framing and Counter-Framing* (New York, N.Y.: Routledge).

28. Farivar Masood (April 30, 2021), "Attacks on Asian Americans Spiked by 164% in First Quarter of 2021," *Voice of America News*, https://www.voanews.com/usa/attacks-asian-americans-spiked-164-first-quarter-2021.

29. Kimmy Yam (March 16, 2021), "There Were 3,800 Anti-Asian Racist Incidents Mostly Against Women in Past Year," *NBC News*, https://www.nbcnews.com/news/asian-america/there-were-3–800-anti-asian-racist-incidents-mostly-against-n1261257.

30. Bill Chappell, Vanessa Romo, and Jaclyn Diaz (March 18, 2021), "Official Who Said Atlanta Shooting Suspect Was Having a 'Bad Day' Face Criticism," *NPR News*, https://www.npr.org/2021/03/17/978141138/atlanta-shooting-suspect-is-believed-to-have-visited-spas-he-targeted.

31. Chester M. Pierce (1980), "Social Trace Contaminants: Subtle Indicators of Racism in TV," in *Television and Social Behavior: Beyond Violence and Children*, ed. S. Wiley and R. Abeles (Hillsdale, N.J.: Lawrence Erlbaum), 251.

32. Ian Haney Lopez (2006), *White by Law: The Legal Construction of Race* (New York, N.Y.: New York University Press).

33. Philomena Essed (1991), *Understanding Everyday Racism: An Interdisciplinary Theory* (Newbury Park, Calif.; Sage).

34. Paige Sweet (2019), "The Sociology of Gaslighting," *American Sociological Review*, *84*(5): 851–875.

35. Angelique M. Davis and Rose Ernst (2019), "Racial Gaslighting," *Politics, Groups, and Identities*, *7*(4): 761–744.

36. Sweet, "The Sociology of Gaslighting."

37. Bonilla- Silva, *Racism Without Racists.*

38. Sullivan, *Good White People*, 87, 96.

Chapter 8. White Women: Oppression Olympics, White Saviors, and Controlling Images

1. Ruth Frankenberg (1993), *White Women, Race Matters* (Minneapolis: University of Minnesota Press).

2. See the following: Mikki Kendall (2020), *Hood Feminism* (New York, N.Y.: Viking); Audre Lorde (1984), *Sister Outsider* (New York, N.Y.: Ten Speed Press); bell hooks (2014), *Feminist Theory: From Margin to Center*, 3rd ed. (New York, N.Y.: Routledge); Ruby Hamad (2020), *White Tears/Brown Scars* (Brooklyn, N.Y.: Catapult).

3. Ange-Marie Hancock (2011), *Solidarity Politics for Millennials: A Guide to Ending the Oppression Olympics* (New York, N.Y.: Palgrave Macmillan); see also Elizabeth Martinez (1998),

De Colores Means All of Us: Latina Views for a Multi-Colored Century (Boston, Mass.: South End Press).

4. Richard Delgado and Jean Stafancic (2012), *Critical Race Theory: An Introduction* (New York, N.Y.: New York University Press).

5. Chester M. Pierce (1995), "Stress Analogs of Racism and Sexism: Terrorism, Torture, and Disaster" in *Mental Health, Racism, and Sexism,* ed. Charles V. White, Patricia Perri Rieker, Bernard M. Karmer, and Bertram S. Brown, 277–293 (Pittsburgh, Pa.: University of Pittsburgh Press).

6. Philomena Essed (2002), "Everyday Racism," in *A Companion to Racial and Ethnic Studies*, ed. by David Theo Goldberg and John Solomos, 202–216 (Malden, Mass.: Blackwell).

7. Ibid., 205.

8. Hancock, *Solidarity Politics for Millennials.*

9. Ibid.

10. Susan B. Anthony House, https://susanbanthonyhouse.org/blog/interpreting-susan-b-anthony-for-our-times/; see also Jessie Daniels (2021), *Nice White Ladies: The Truth About White Supremacy, Our Role in It, and How We Can Help Dismantle It* (New York, N.Y.: Seal Press).

11. Hancock, *Solidarity Politics for Millennials.*

12. Lorde, *Sister Outsider* (New York, N.Y.: Ten Speed Press), Letter to Mary Daly.

13. Ibid., The Use of Anger.

14. Eduardo Bonilla- Silva (2022), *Racism Without Racists: Colorblind Racism and the Persistence of Racial Inequality in America*, 6th ed. (Lanham, Md.: Rowman & Littlefield).

15. Patricia Hill Collins (2000), *Black Feminist Thought: Knowledge, Consciousness and the Politics of Empowerment* (New York, N.Y.: Routledge).

16. Emily Cataneo (October 14, 2020), "A Brief History of the Women's KKK," *JSTOR Daily*, https://daily.jstor.org/a-brief-history-of-the-womens-kkk/.

17. Stephanie E. Jones-Rogers (2020), *They Were Her Property* (New Haven, Conn.: Yale University Press).

18. Evelyn Nakano Glenn (2002), *Unequal Freedom: How Race and Gender Shaped American Citizenship and Labor* (Cambridge, Mass.: Harvard University Press).

19. Hamad, *White Tears/Brown Scars*, 97.

20. Richard Dyer (2005), "The Matter of Whiteness," in *White Privilege: Essential Readings on the Other Side of Racism*, ed. P. S. Rothenberg, 9–14 (New York, N.Y.: Worth).

21. Matma Motwani Accapadi (2007), "When White Women Cry: How White Women's Tears Oppress Women of Color," *College Student Affairs Journal, 26*(2): 208–215.

22. Video retrieved from https://heavy.com/news/2018/05/jennifer-schulte-bbq-becky/.

23. Frankenberg, *White Women, Race Matters.*

24. Hamad, *White Tears/Brown Scars*, 99.

25. Ibid.

26. Collins, *Black Feminist Thought.*

27. Marianne Bertrand and Sendhil Mullainathan (2004), "Are Emily and Greg More Employable than Lakisha and Jamal? A Field Experiment on Labor Market Discrimination," *American Economic Review, 94*(4): 991–1013.

28. Stephanie Bornstein (2022), "Confronting the Racial Pay Gap," *Vanderbilt Law Review, 75*: 1401–1460.

29. Ibid.

30. Shannon Sullivan (2006), *Revealing Whiteness: The Unconscious Habits of Racial Privilege* (Bloomington: Indiana University Press).

31. Brittany Aronson (2017), "The White Savior Industrial Complex: A Cultural Studies Analysis of a Teacher Educator, Savior Film, and Future Teachers," *Journal of Critical Thought and Praxis*, *6*(3): 36–45. See also Teju Cole's (2012) response to Kony (2012). Teju Cole (March 21, 2012), "The White-Savior Industrial Complex." *The Atlantic*, https://www.theatlantic.com/international/archive/2012/03/the-white-savior-industrial-complex/254843.

32. Hamad, *White Tears/Brown Scars*, 151.

33. Brittany Aronson (2017), "The White Savior Industrial Complex: A Cultural Studies Analysis of a Teacher Educator, Savior Film, and Future Teachers," *Journal of Critical Thought and Praxis*, *6*(3): 37.

34. Chester M. Pierce (1970), "Offensive Mechanisms," in *The Black Seventies*, ed. Floyd B. Barbour (Boston Mass.: Porter Sargent), 274.

35. Ibid.

36. Hamad, *White Tears/Brown Scars*; see also Edward Said (1978), *Orientalism* (New York, N.Y.: Random House).

37. Derald Wing Sue, Jennifer Bucceri, Annie I. Lin, Kevin L. Nadal, and Gina C. Torino (2007), "Racial Microaggressions and the Asian American Experience," *Cultural Diversity and Ethnic Minority Psychology*, *13*(1): 72–81.

38. Rosalind Chou (2012), *Asian American Sexual Politics* (Lanham, Md.: Rowman & Littlefield).

39. Pierce, "Offensive Mechanisms," 272.

40. June E. Cook (1977), "Microaggressions and Classroom Social Interaction in Three Inner-City High Schools" (PhD diss., Union Graduate School for Experimenting Colleges and University).

41. Rosalind Chou and Joe Feagin (2008), *The Myth of the Model Minority: Asian Americans Facing Racism* (Boulder, Colo.: Paradigm).

42. Mia Tuan (1999), *Forever Foreigners or Honorary Whites? The Asian Ethnic Experience Today* (New Brunswick, N.J.: Rutgers University Press).

43. Bonilla- Silva, *Racism Without Racists*.

44. Joe R. Feagin (2013), *The White Racial Frame: Centuries of Racial Framing and Counter-Framing* (New York, N.Y.: Routledge).

45. Rosina Lippi-Green (2011), *English with an Accent: Language, Ideology, and Discrimination in the United States* (New York, N.Y.: Routledge).

Chapter 9. White Sexual Imperialism and White Men

1. Alexis Stevens and Shaddi Abusaid (March 17, 2021), "'A Crime Against Us All': Outrage, Grief After Deadly Spa Shootings," *Atlanta Journal Constitution*, https://www.ajc.com/news/exclusive-spa-shooting-suspect-bought-gun-hours-before-deadly-spree/FEURWVYBEFBMJP7GLOQ6AQJ27A/.

2. Ji-yoon Hwang (March 17, 2021), "Atlanta Shooter Says He Will Kill All Asians," *Chosun Ilbo*, https://www.chosun.com/international/us/2021/03/17/XSDXYLMAQZCC5JWMQ4HGRZGOG4/.

3. Hanna Park (April 2, 2021), "He Shot at 'Everyone He Saw': Atlanta Spa Workers Recount Horrors of Shooting," *NBC News*, https://www.nbcnews.com/news/asian-america/he-shot-everyone-he-saw-atlanta-spa-workers-recount-horrors-n1262928.

4. Guardian Staff (March 17, 2021), "Georgia Officer Condemned for Saying Atlanta Shooter Was 'Having a Bad Day,'" *The Guardian*, https://www.theguardian.com/us-news/2021/mar/17/jay-baker-bad-day-t-shirt-atlanta-spa-shooting.

5. Patricia Hill Collins (2000), *Black Feminist Thought: Knowledge, Consciousness and the Politics of Empowerment* (New York, N.Y.: Routledge). See also Angela Y. Davis (1981), *Women, Race, and Class* (New York, N.Y.: Random House).

6. Elizabeth A. Mosley, Jessica R. Prince, Grace B. McKee, Sierra E. Carter, Ruschelle M. Leone, Kathy Gill-Hopple, and Amanda K. Gilmore (2021), "Racial Disparities in Sexual Assault Characteristics and Mental Health Care After Sexual Assault Medical Forensic Exams," *Journal of Women's Health*, *30*(10): 1448–1456. See also Jameta Nicole Barlow (February 1, 2020), "Black Women, the Forgotten Survivors of Sexual Assault," American Psychological Association, https://www.apa.org/topics/sexual-assault-harassment/black-women-sexual-violence.

7. Brittany C. Slatton and April L. Richard (2020), "Black Women's Experiences of Sexual Assault and Disclosure: Insights from the Margins," *Sociology Compass*, *14*(6).

8. Celine Parrañez Shimizu (2006), *The Hypersexuality of Race: Performing Asian/American Women on Screen and Scene* (Durham, N.C.: Duke University Press).

9. Elaine Kim (1990), "'Such Opposite Creatures':" Men and Women in Asian American Literature," *Michigan Quarterly Review*, *29*: 68–93.

10. Edward Said (1978), *Orientalism* (New York, N.Y.: Random House).

11. Robin Zheng (2016), "Why Yellow Fever Isn't Flattering: A Case Against Racial Fetishes," *Journal of the American Philosophical Association*, 2(3): 400–419.

12. Sunny Woan (2008), "White Sexual Imperialism: A Theory of Asian Feminist Jurisprudence," *Washington and Lee Journal of Civil Rights and Social Justice*, *14*(2): 275–301.

13. Julie Yuki Ralston (1998), "Geishas, Gays, and Grunts: What the Exploitation of Asian Pacific Women Reveals About Military Culture and the Legal Ban on Lesbian, Gay, and Bisexual Service Members," *Minnesota Journal of Law and Inequality*, *16*(2): 661–711.

14. Woan, "White Sexual Imperialism."

15. Aki Uchida (1998), "The Orientalization of Asian Women in America," *Women's Studies International Forum*, *21*(2): 161–174.

16. Ibid.

17. Robert E. Hall (2004), "Entitlement Disorder: The Colonial Traditions of Power as White Male Resistance to Affirmative Action," *Journal of Black Studies*, *34*(4): 562–579.

18. Collins, *Black Feminist Thought*.

19. Rosalind Chou (2012), *Asian American Sexual Politics* (Lanham, Md.: Rowman & Littlefield), 92–94.

20. Miranda Fricker (2007), *Epistemic Injustice: Power and the Ethics of Knowing* (New York, N.Y.: Oxford University Press).

21. Chester M. Pierce (1970), "Offensive Mechanisms," in *The Black Seventies*, ed. Floyd B. Barbour, 265–282 (Boston, Mass.: Porter Sargent).

22. Joane Nagel (2003), *Race, Ethnicity, and Sexuality: Intimate Intersections, Forbidden Frontiers* (New York, N.Y.: Oxford University Press).

23. Jade Jackman (April 11, 2018), "The Meme Account Hilariously Exposing Asian Fetish Guys on Tinder," *Vice*, https://www.vice.com/en/article/kzxpdn/fleshlight-chronicles-asian-fetish-tinder-memes.

24. Dresden Lackey and Rosalind Chou (2019), "Foreign, Fetishized, Fever! An Examination of the Exotification of Asian and Asian American Women by White Men in the U.S.," in *The Yellow Book*, ed. Isaac Chong, 283–302 (Berlin: He Xiangyu Studio). See also Chou, *Asian American Sexual Politics*.

25. Nagel, *Race, Ethnicity, and Sexuality*.

26. Bill Chappell, Vanessa Romo, and Jaclyn Diaz (March 18, 2021), "Official Who Said Atlanta Shooting Suspect Was Having a 'Bad Day' Face Criticism," *NPR News*, https://www.npr.org/2021/03/17/978141138/atlanta-shooting-suspect-is-believed-to-have-visited-spas-he-targeted.

27. Ruth Frankenberg (1993), *White Women, Race Matters* (Minneapolis: University of Minnesota Press).

28. Sumi K. Cho (2003), "Converging Stereotypes in Racialized Sexual Harassment: Where the Model Minority Meets Suzie Wong," in *Critical Race Feminisms*, ed. Adrien Katherine Wing (New York, N.Y.: New York University Press).

29. Woan, "White Sexual Imperialism," 294.

30. Wei-Chin Hwang (2013), "Who Are People Willing to Date? Ethnic and Gender Patterns in Online Dating," *Race and Social Problems*, *5*: 28–40.

31. Patricia Hill Collins (2004), *Black Sexual Politics: African Americans, Gender, and the New Racism* (New York, N.Y.: Routledge).

32. Anna Kelsey-Sugg and Marc Fennell (November 16, 2021), "The Fight for Sarah Baartman," *Stuff the British Stole*, https://www.abc.net.au/news/2021–11–17/stuff-the-british-stole-sarah-baartman-south-africa-london/100568276.

33. Collins, *Black Sexual Politics*.

34. Sadiah Qureshi (2004), "Displaying Sarah Baartman, the 'Hottentot Venus,'" *History of Science*, *42*(2): 233–257.

35. Collins, *Black Sexual Politics*.

36. Philomena Essed (2008), "Everyday Racism," in *A Companion to Racial and Ethnic Studies*, ed. David Theo Goldberg and John Solomos, chap. 15 (Hoboken, N.J.: Wiley).

37. Dorothy Roberts (1997), *Killing the Black Body: Race, Reproduction, and the Meaning of Liberty* (New York, N.Y.: Penguin Random House); Thomas Jefferson (1832), *Notes on the State of Virginia* (Boston, Mass.: Lilly and Wait), originally published 1785; George M. Fredrickson (2016), *Racism: A Short History* (Princeton, N.J.: Princeton University Press).

38. Dorothy Roberts (2011), *Fatal Invention: How Science, Politics, and Big Business Re-Create Race in the Twenty-First Century* (New York, N.Y.: New Press).

39. bell hooks (1992), *Black Looks: Race and Representation* (New York, N.Y.: Routledge).

Chapter 10. "It's Ontological": Moving Forward in Understanding Microaggressions

1. Jemima McEvoy (July 22, 2020), "Sales of 'White Fragility'—and Other Anti-Racism Books—Jumped over 2000% After Protests Began," *Forbes*, https://www.forbes.com/sites/jemimamcevoy/2020/07/22/sales-of-white-fragility-and-other-anti-racism-books-jumped-over-2000-after-protests-began/?sh=67852c7f303d.

2. Andrea Hsu (January 23, 2025), "Trump Calls DEI Programs 'Illegal.' He Plans to End Them in the Federal Government," *NPR News*, https://www.npr.org/2025/01/23/nx-s1-5271588/trump-dei-diversity-equity-inclusion-federal-workers-government.

3. Te-Ping Chen and Lauren Weber (July 21, 2023), "The Rise and Fall of the Chief Diversity Officer," *Wall Street Journal*, https://www.wsj.com/business/c-suite/chief-diversity-officer-cdo-business-corporations-e110a82f.

4. Derrick Bell (1992), *Faces at the Bottom of the Well* (New York, N.Y.: Basic Books).

5. Silvia Domínguez and David G. Embrick (2020), "Racial Microaggressions: Bridging Psychology and Sociology and Future Research Considerations," *Sociology Compass*, *14*(8): 1–14. See also Jioni A. Lewis, Ruby Mendenhall, Stacy A. Harwood, and Margaret Browne Huntt (2013), "Coping with Gendered Racial Microaggressions Among Black Women College Students," *Journal of African American Studies*, *17*: 51–73.

6. Chester M. Pierce (1974), "Psychiatric Problems of the Black Minority," in *American Handbook of Psychiatry*, ed. S. Arieti, 512–523 (New York, N.Y.: Basic Books).

7. Chester M. Pierce (1995), "Stress Analogs of Racism and Sexism: Terrorism, Torture, and Disaster," in *Mental Health, Racism, and Sexism*, ed. Charles V. White, Patricia Perri Rieker, Bernard M. Karmer, and Bertram S. Brown, 277–293 (Pittsburgh, Pa.: University of Pittsburgh Press).

8. Audre Lorde (1984), *Sister Outsider* (New York, N.Y.: Ten Speed Press).

9. Susan Bordo (1993), "Feminism, Foucault, and the Politics of the Body," in *Up Against Foucault*, ed. C. Ramazanoglu, 170–202 (New York, N.Y.: Routledge).

10. Johnny E. Williams and David G. Embrick (2023), "Moving Beyond Obfuscating Racial Microaggression Discourse," *Social Inclusion*, *11*(2): 5–15.

11. Ibid., 11.

12. Pierce, "Psychiatric Problems of the Black Minority."

13. Richard Delgado and Jean Stafancic (2012), *Critical Race Theory: An Introduction* (New York, N.Y.: New York University Press).

14. Philomena Essed (1991), *Understanding Everyday Racism: An Interdisciplinary Theory* (Newbury Park, Calif.: Sage).

15. Philomena Essed (2008), "Everyday Racism," in *A Companion to Racial and Ethnic Studies*, ed. David Theo Goldberg and John Solomos (Hoboken, N.J.: Wiley), 214.

INDEX

abstract liberalism, 18
American-born Chinese (ABC), 48–49, 50, 76
American descendants of slavery (ADOS), 13, 52, 53, 76
Anderson, Elijah, 78
Angry Black Woman, 42, 53, 61, 64, 100–101, 120
Anthony, Susan B., 95, 96
assimilation, 26, 49; to American cultural norms, 32, 36, 37, 38, 46, 48; to whiteness, 28, 29, 30, 36, 43, 71, 72

Baartman, Sarah, 120
Bell, Derrick, 3, 125
Black Matriarch, 19, 60
Bonilla-Silva, Eduardo, 12, 18, 20, 23, 79, 82, 84, 90
Bordo, Susan, 127–128
Brunsma, David, 78

China doll, 20, 83, 104
Chou, Rosalind, 31, 81, 117
Clark, Kenneth, 81
Clark, Mamie, 81
co-ethnic spaces, 12–13, 26, 28, 35, 51, 70, 79, 88–89
Collins, Patricia Hill, 12, 19, 20, 22, 23, 101, 120
colonialism, 30, 79, 118, 122; effect on Asian women of, 32, 113; "mental colonialization," 71; sexism and, 61, 64–65; white supremacy and, 3, 6, 36, 39, 114
color blindness, 3, 12, 14, 16–18, 23, 86, 89, 91, 106–109, 126; color-blind parenting, 79–84; weaponization of, 96–99, 100
colorism, 27, 39–43, 55, 66
compassion deficit disorder, 96
Connell, R. W., 31
controlling images, 17, 23, 56–57, 122; of Asian women, 22, 47, 48, 87, 116, 117; of Black women, 22, 33–34, 42, 47, 50, 53, 120; bodies and, 60, 61–62, 64; definition of, 19–20; internalization of, 49, 51, 54, 73; whiteness and, 46–51, 59, 100–109, 112, 113, 119. *See also* Angry Black Woman, Black Matriarch, China doll, Jezebel, Lotus Blossom, welfare queens
coping mechanisms, 13. *See also* resilience, resistance
counterframes, 14, 17
counterspaces, 78–79
critical race feminism, 12, 13, 21, 23, 128
critical race theory, 3, 21, 45, 89, 125, 128
Crouch, Maria, 75
Crutchfield, Jandel, 39
cultural racism, 18, 20

Dang, Tran, 47
David, E. J. R., 75
Davis, Angelique, 90
Davis, Shardé, 51
defiant ignorance, 96, 98
Derthick, E. J. R. Annie, 72
DiAngelo, Robin, 125
double consciousness, 44, 49, 117
Douglass, Frederick, 16
Dragon Lady, 20, 101, 113, 117
Du Bois, W. E. B., 16, 49, 117
Dunn, Chelsie, 64
Dyer, Richard, 99

Embrick, David, 128
Ernst, Rose, 90
Essed, Philomena, 4–5, 8, 10, 14, 21–22, 26, 95, 111–112, 121, 129
exceptional belonging, 82
exotification, 56, 72, 127; of Asian women, 22, 104, 112–113, 116, 118, 119, 122; of Black women, 120–121, 122

Fanon, Frantz, 72
Fatphobia, 63–66
Feagin, Joe, 12, 14, 16, 20, 23, 27, 75, 81
femininity: hegemonic femininity, 60–61; white femininity, 60–61, 63
forever foreign, 38, 46, 48, 50, 87, 88, 105, 106, 107, 112, 116
Frankenberg, Ruth, 35
fresh off the boat (FOB), 48, 76
Fricker, Miranda, 117

Hall, J. Camille, 39
Hall, Ronald E., 114
Hamad, Ruby, 71, 98, 100, 102
Hamilton, Charles, 16
Hancock, Ange-Marie, 95
hermeneutical injustice, 117
heteronormativity, 114, 115; compulsory heterosexuality, 31, 115
Higginbotham, Evelyn Brooks, 68
Hood, Kristina, 64
hooks, bell, 15, 61, 94
Hughey, Matthew, 31
Hwang, Wei-Chin, 120
hypersexuality, 53, 61, 62, 66, 101, 112, 115

identity politics, 43
imperialism, 30, 122; sexual imperialism, 113, 114, 117–119; U.S. involvement in Asian countries, 34; as white supremacy, 3, 6, 32, 36, 39, 102
individualism, 47, 51, 56, 81, 101, 118, 122
internalized racism, 3, 29, 33, 71–76
intersectionality, 12, 13, 14, 75, 83, 87, 90, 102, 115; and critical race feminism, 19–21; and Oppression Olympics, 96, 97, 98.

Jezebel, 19, 60, 62, 72, 101, 112, 115, 119
Johnston, Marc, 46

Kendell, Mikki, 94
Kim, Claire Jean, 6–7
Koval, Christy, 68–69

Laybourn, SunAh, 82
leapfrog paranoia, 95
Lipsitz, George, 44
Lorde, Audre, 22, 94, 96, 127
Lotus Blossom, 20, 60, 63, 101, 104, 112, 113, 117, 119

Mammy, 19, 22, 102
Marshall, Annecka, 62
Martínez, Elizabeth, 84
masculinity: hegemonic masculinity, 31; white masculinity, 31, 61
matrix of domination, 12, 20–22, 76, 83
Mills, Charles W., 16
model minority myth, 11, 52, 53, 74, 87, 88
movement backlash, 95
mythical norm, 22

Nadal, Kevin, 46
naturalization, 18
neoliberalism, 3, 14, 96
ontological expansiveness, 51, 54–55, 102

Oppression Olympics, 84, 86, 94–100, 109, 122
Orientalism, 32, 84–88, 91, 113, 116, 118, 119
Owens, Bianca, 64

Pérez, Lindsay, 74
Petalio, Jessica, 75
Pierce, Chester, 9–10; conceptualization of microaggressions, 4, 6, 7–8, 26, 70, 71, 88, 103–104, 111–112; in conversation with other scholars, 5, 9, 12, 14, 19, 39, 95, 104, 117, 128; examples of microaggressions, 28, 36, 46; internalized white supremacy, 35, 44, 51, 53, 72, 75, 127
Pyke, Karen, 47, 72

racial gaslighting, 36, 90–91, 117, 128
racial realism, 3, 4, 126
racial spectacles, 90
racialized other, 5, 9, 44, 105, 109, 118–122
racism *See* cultural racism; internalized racism; systemic racism
resilience, 13, 127
resistance, 13, 15, 78, 127–128
respectability politics, 43, 62, 68
Reyes, Victoria, 11
Rich, Adrienne, 31, 115
Rienzi, Elizabeth, 80, 82
Rosette, Ashleigh, 68–69

Said, Edward, 113
Schippers, Mimi, 60
Shiao, Jiannbin, 80, 82
slavery, 3, 13, 39, 98, 121; effect on women, 61, 69, 112, 114; as precursor to modern racism, 6, 16, 17, 30, 52, 80, 122. *See also* American descendants of slavery (ADOS)
Solórzano, Daniel, 74
Strings, Sabrina, 63, 64
Sue, Derald Wing, 4, 7, 10, 19, 28–29, 35, 53, 104
Sullivan, Shannon, 9, 51, 54, 82, 102
Sweet, Paige, 90
systemic racism, 3, 33, 47, 69, 80, 106–107, 125; alienation and, 29, 39, 51–52; definition of, 16–18, 27; white supremacy and, 6, 17, 20

texturism, 27, 66–69
thin privilege, 59
Tuan, Mia, 80, 82
Ture, Kwame, 16

unjust enrichment, 16, 17, 27, 29, 80, 114

welfare queens, 19, 22, 51, 101
Wells-Barnett, Ida B., 16
white habitus, 75, 78, 89, 90, 91
white racial frame, 12, 13, 14, 55, 81, 102, 105, 107, 113, 119, 122, 126, 128; bodies and, 63, 64, 66–68; color-blind ideology and, 79, 85, 91; definition of, 16–18; and patriarchy, 26–27, 31, 32, 62, 70; as tool for white supremacy, 6, 26–27, 29, 36, 51, 71–72, 75, 76, 99, 100. *See also* counterframes
white saviorism, 100–108, 122, 126; white savior industrial complex 102
white space, 11, 26, 51, 70, 91, 116, 126; belonging and, 89, 90, 97; definition of, 78–79
whiteness: desire for, 12, 27–30; honorary whiteness, 82, 104
willful blindness, 95, 97–98, 100
Williams, Johnny, 128
Woan, Sunny, 113, 119

X, Malcolm, 72

www.ingramcontent.com/pod-product-compliance
Lightning Source LLC
Chambersburg PA
CBHW020939090926
51106CB00053B/772
* 9 7 8 0 8 2 0 3 7 5 7 5 5 *